Making Governance
Work

Total Quality Education for the World's Best Schools

The Comprehensive Planning and Implementation Guide for School Administrators

Series Editor: **Larry E. Frase**

The authors dedicate this series to the memory of
W. Edwards Deming, 1900-1993

Making Governance Work

TQE for School Boards

William K. Poston Jr.

CORWIN PRESS, INC.
A Sage Publications Company
Thousand Oaks, California

For information address:

Corwin Press, Inc.
A Sage Publications Company
2455 Teller Road
Thousand Oaks, California 91320

SAGE Publications Ltd.
6 Bonhill Street
London EC2A 4PU
United Kingdom

SAGE Publications India Pvt. Ltd.
M-32 Market
Greater Kailash I
New Delhi 110 048 India

Library of Congress Cataloging-in-Publication Data

Poston, William K. Jr.
    Making governance work : total quality education for school boards /
William K. Poston Jr.
        p. cm. — (Total quality education for the world's best schools , v. 8)
    Includes bibliographical references.
    ISBN 0–8039–6144–8 (pbk. : alk. paper)
        1. School boards—United States. 2. Educational leadership—
United States. 3. Total quality management—United States.
    I. Title. II. Series.
    LB2831.P67   1994
    379.1′531′0973—dc20   93–47928

    99 00 01 02 03 04 05 10 9 8 7 6 5 4 3

Corwin Press Production Editor: Marie Louise Penchoen

Contents

Foreword

Consider where our country is now in the world order, dethroned as the world's greatest economic power. Think about the alleged deteriorating morals in today's society. Think about

1. Claims that an ever-increasing number of adults cannot read
2. Declining achievement scores
3. Ever-increasing numbers of single-parent families
4. Devastating effects of the HIV virus
5. Children who come to school hungry
6. Industries' claims that students are coming to them with woefully inadequate skills to perform jobs
7. Disruptive labor relations between teachers, administrators, and school boards
8. Violence announced on every front page of every newspaper nearly every day

Can any single agency resolve all of these problems? Now, think about school boards. They are expected to resolve these problems as they pertain to students. Every state in the U.S. assigns the responsibility for education—and for correcting all these problems—to school boards. Nearly every state also determines how much money can be spent on education; determines which courses must be taught; certifies teachers and administrators for hiring; provides tenure to teachers and, in some states, administrators; prescribes budgeting procedures and building requirements; and directs schools to cure our social ills. Unfortunately, as the boards' duties have grown throughout the 20th century, the latitude to perform them has decreased.

School board governance is now far more difficult than it once was. The stakes are higher, and the degrees of freedom to attain them are far more restricted. School board members must now be extremely knowledgeable about their responsibilities: effective governance and labor relations, sound financial practices, and firm knowledge of politics and the law, among others.

Yet the one responsibility the state lawmaking bodies forgot to assign to boards is training. Board members, whether they are businesspeople, homemakers, or postal workers, are simply elected and thrown into their jobs. It is not unreasonable that many newspapers and books demean the performance of school boards. They are given the toughest job of all without the training or freedom needed to succeed.

Training is what this book is about. The author, William K. Poston Jr., has served as superintendent of three school districts ranging in size from 4,000 to 20,000 students, over a 25-year period in administration. He has experienced labor relations problems and board meeting rooms filled with frantic and vociferous parents. He has faced nearly every challenge known to school boards and superintendents, and he has written numerous books and professional articles dealing with a multitude of school governance problems. Professor Poston knows school governance. *Making Governance Work* should be read by every school board member and superintendent who wants to learn from these challenges.

Instead of listing platitudes and obvious rules, this book provides the contexts in which many educational problems occur, including the insights and tools needed to address them. Professor Poston expertly explains the governance role of boards and the tools and skills members must have for fulfilling them.

School board members face incredible challenges and responsibilities. The future of U.S. education rests heavily on their shoulders. This book will ease their burden considerably.

Larry E. Frase
San Diego State University

Preface

Schools are governed by elected or appointed lay members of a community. Every day, school board members make decisions that affect the performance and the operations of school districts. However, without valid and complete information, board decision-making may be seriously impeded or ineffective. Valid and complete information is vital to accurate and sound problem identification, issue analysis, and selection of appropriate action by school boards. Total Quality Education (TQE) offers an instructive body of research information about a promising process for school boards seeking to establish and continually improve quality in their school organizations.

This book, *Making Governance Work: TQE for School Boards* is designed for practicing school board members, and it is structured to be of help to busy board members who look for guidance and assistance with the complex tasks and responsibilities of school governance needed for high-quality school systems. The book provides a selective, research-focused body of information about board roles in key areas related to successful school governance, grounded in principles of system quality improvement. Given adequate and appropriate knowledge, informed board members may be better equipped to deal with the diverse and challenging demands that confront their schools.

The Promise of Quality Philosophy

The promise of the quality improvement philosophy is to enhance and to improve the schooling provided to learners across this country. No task is more significant or important for school boards than that of improving the quality of teaching and learning steadily over time. At the same time, no task is more elusive, confusing, or difficult to grasp. Schools are burdened with diminishing resources, rapidly changing clientele, rising public expectations, and, occasionally, ineffective tools and leadership.

As W. Edwards Deming (1982) states, "Quality begins with the intent, which is fixed by management" (p. 5). Accordingly, the job of quality improvement begins with the school board, and board governance must be done and done well. Board members for the most part want to make "right" and lasting contributions to the benefit of the system and clientele, and that is the underlying focus of this book.

Total Quality Education is more than a set of suggestions—it is a new philosophy drawn from the profound knowledge taught by W. Edwards Deming and others. More than that, it is a set of beliefs and values translated into organizational actions that promote and foster the improvement of schools. The elements of this new philosophy center on (a) removing the causes of problems to improve productivity, (b) involving people and workers in improving teaching and learning so that each feels like a valued contributor, and (c) using knowledge of systems to make changes that enhance the functioning of the schools. Greater detail about this new philosophy is found in chapter 2, but board members need to know that their job in this new philosophy is to promote a sound organizational design that is suitable to meet the school's needs and to establish consistency of performance in delivery within the system. Every organization, even the good ones, can improve given the tools, the commitment, and the processes necessary for the task. It is hoped that these elements advance the purpose of this book.

Purpose of This Book

The purpose of this book is threefold:

1. To foster board member understanding and command of the complex issues of Total Quality Education and its relationship to school governance
2. To provide clues, contexts, and content critical to the enhancement of school system quality within the responsibilities of school boards
3. To establish a framework for long-term focus on educational advancement and improvement through Total Quality Education

Board members who are interested in obtaining a road map for comprehensive improvement in their school system should find this book useful. Moreover, the book has been carefully based on research and practitioner literature focused on the core of sound school board management, policies, and operations.

Board Member Roles and Responsibilities

Board members are usually elected officials, chosen by their communities to represent them in managing and supervising the community's schools. Board selection is primarily a democratic process, resulting in a body of government considered closer to the people than most other forms of government in a democracy. Board service is not an easy task. In addition, democratic representation is very complex, time-consuming, and difficult at best. Nevertheless, it is probably the best form of governance that exists among free societies. ("Democracy," as Winston Churchill is supposed to have said, "is the worst form of government known to history, save for all the others.") Board members, in serving to deliver democratic governance, have a huge need for accurate knowledge and information. It goes without saying that the better the information a board has, the better their decisions, and correspondingly, the better their success and quality of governance.

Crises result as the consequence of poor prior planning and preparation. Boards must be prepared and plan for quality school systems. Quality is seldom an accident.

School boards are unique institutional bodies in American culture, and the job of serving as a board member is often perplexing and laborious. New requirements, changing societal expectations, revolutionary alterations of family and other institutions, and emerging social and economic factors and demands create a climate of uncertainty and fluctuations in organizational direction. Board members are hard-pressed to know what is best for schools, and they often feel unprepared to deal with some of the problems and issues that confront them. They need answers to tough questions, and they often do not have the time it takes to acquire appropriate understanding of complicated issues on their own. This book provides a comprehensive compilation of information on complicated issues that face board members and is organized for easy access to tools and data needed for the boards' roles and responsibilities. The content was collected and coordinated for busy board members seeking background and additional learnings on governance, management, educational events and problems, and procedures to improve schools.

The quality of school governance at the local level depends on sincere individuals who are committed to giving time, energy, work, judgment, and diligent commitment to quality. However, few rewards accrue to board members for making such sacrifices. Nevertheless, American schools for the most part have developed under sound lay leadership provided by elected boards. Perhaps this is due to the tradition of electing board members generally from the "mainstream" of the community and to the serious attention to responsibility provided by board members who have been invested with the trust and confidence of neighbors and community colleagues. By and large, local school board members take their responsibilities very seriously. When issues confront them, they carefully analyze the nature and characteristics of the issue, deliberate collaboratively as to findings and possible courses of action, and render appropriate judgments in accordance with the information and their understandings. The process is sound, and it is to help with that process that this book is dedicated.

Next Steps for School Board Members

This book does not provide all that anyone needs to know to be an effective member of a high-performance board. However, it does provide enough of the "right stuff" to help a sincere and busy public servant begin planning for Total Quality Education and to further his or her own self-education and personal development to do the right things in behalf of children, schools, and communities. If this compilation of research and practice helps one board member improve the quality of his or her school system, then this effort will have been a success.

This book is directed at improving and enhancing school governance by providing board members and others with some tools of informed judgment and system functioning. Board members' interest in improving America's schools may be boundless, and there are probably many sources of information germane to education, research about what works and does not work in schools, and writings about how to effectively do things that need to be done in schools. This book pulls together many of those important ideas and research findings on school quality development and improvement to give boards an overview of the broad picture and many of the delicate details of sound school governance. It is neither the last word, nor is it all-inclusive. However, if used as a guide to understanding and further study, it will provide board members with a tool to advance the quality of their school system. If it is used properly, both this book and board members will have contributed to a significant accomplishment: the improvement of American schooling for future generations. . . .

William K. Poston Jr.
Iowa State University

Reference

Deming, W. E. (1982). *Out of the crisis*. Cambridge: MIT Press.

About the Author

William K. Poston Jr. is currently Associate Professor of Educational Administration in the Department of Professional Studies at Iowa State University in Ames, Iowa. He is an experienced administrator, with 25 years of experience in school administration, including 15 years as a superintendent in the Flowing Wells (Tucson) and Kyrene (Tempe-Phoenix) Schools in Arizona and in the Billings Public Schools in Montana. He earned his B.A. at the University of Northern Iowa and his Ed.S. and Ed.D. at Arizona State University. He has many distinctive professional achievements, including service as the youngest-elected international president of Phi Delta Kappa and selection as an Outstanding Young Leader in American Education.

At Iowa State University, he currently teaches courses in Total Quality Education, strategic planning, school business management, school finance, contract negotiations, and superintendent-school board relationships. In addition to his professorial responsibilities, he directs the Iowa Superintendents' Academy and the Iowa School Business Management Academy, both of which are professional development and advanced certification programs for administrators in Iowa. He is author of over 50 journal articles and publications on topics of educational reform, educational quality auditing, and performance-based budgeting and decision making. He is an active consultant to school systems across the country, and he has authored the book, *Making Schools Work: Practical Management of School Operations.*

William K. Poston Jr. was certified as a lead curriculum auditor by the National Curriculum Audit Center after completion of the inaugural training class in Montreal, Canada in 1988, and he has participated in 21 school system curriculum management audits, with service as the lead auditor on 18 audits.

✧ **1** ✧

Board Governance and Change

School boards have been reported in recent years to be "in trouble." This time-honored, venerable public institution has shown evidence of eroding support, flagging performance, and political confusion. Although the public believes in the need for school boards, the public has little understanding of how boards actually work. Ironically, the public also has surprisingly little interest in electing or supporting board members (Peirce, 1986). Moreover, grassroots, local control of schools has been threatened by state policy shifts and mushrooming external mandates. The immense wave of reform during the past decade has left board members behind, despite the central role that board members play in fostering and supporting changes in the schools under their charge.

Against this backdrop, many changes recommended for school districts have emerged. It is ironic that recommendations seemed to emerge from the belief that boards have not been doing a good job in delivering quality education (Leone, 1992). One report on school board governance indicated that school boards have been isolated from mainstream community demands and needs (Institute for Educational Leadership, 1986). As a result, school boards appear to be a prime target of public clamor for a better return on investment in public schooling.

- Declining public financial and operational support for schools
- Changing demographic composition of clientele and society
- Perceived drops in student achievement levels and school performance
- Persistent and exorbitant school attrition or dropouts
- Complex social problems, including youth pregnancy, suicide, sexually transmitted diseases, and so on.
- Threats to safety and well-being of schools, with increases in acts of violence
- Labor union demands and adversarial relationships with employee groups
- Outmoded, or obsolescent curricula, thought to be less than adequate in preparing youth for a complex economic workplace
- Failure of U.S. students to compete with students from other countries

Exhibit 1.1. Contemporary Issues Facing School Boards

Issues Facing Boards

Remarkably, school boards may be the best hope for improvement of quality in public schools despite their uncomfortably severe challenges and faltering credibility. Educational issues of many stripes have emerged in the past decade to challenge board members. The impact of thorny, complex changes in the American educational culture has created a stage for board members to play new roles. Some key issues manifested from societal and cultural change, not in any priority order, are listed in Exhibit 1.1. Considerable interest and strong public reaction to these issues have produced a fresh appraisal of the role and effectiveness of public schools.

Initiatives for School Boards

The demand for better school system results in the face of persistent challenges at home and abroad requires delving deeply into core values, questioning basic assumptions, and exploring options and alternatives. Making comprehensive, meaningful change in the complex, interconnected systems of schools, board members could never have too much information. Despite claims to the contrary, most efforts at change in schools tackle only a part of the problem. However, schools are not simple organizations. Diverse and complex forces in schools stand in the way of responding to isolated strategies for improvement. Some simplistic solutions have been proposed in recent years, including teacher empowerment, decentralization of school decision making, competition between schools for enrollment, and so on (Goens & Clover, 1992). However, changing schools is not simple, nor is it singular in nature. Schools embody vast numbers of client needs and characteristics, unique and plentiful expectations from every corner of society, and immense interconnections of sociopolitical forces influencing the goals of the system.

Grappling with what to do first has become more of a challenge to school boards than how to do what it is that needs to be done. School boards must face the challenges and demands, adapt to new initiatives and requirements from clientele, and modify the organizational functions and programs to fulfill their responsibilities.

Several areas have been identified as in need of attention. In a 1990 study conducted by Phi Delta Kappa, the areas listed in rank order in Exhibit 1.2 were rated as both important and inadequate by at least half of the study's educational leader-respondents (Williams, 1990). These problems and issues were not only identified as in need of additional clarification and illumination for boards and superintendents, but strong suggestions were included in the study calling for information to remedy the paucity of understanding. Board member concerns in a previous study were similar (Institute for Educational Leadership, 1986). The top seven issues at that time are enumerated in Exhibit 1.3.

1. Budgeting and finance
2. Social issues
3. Legal problems
4. Board-superintendent relationships
5. Ethics
6. Personnel evaluation
7. Policy development

Exhibit 1.2. Problems Listed by School Leaders in Rank Order

Given the erosion of political support for schools, it is nonetheless surprising to note that challenges to effectiveness of school boards are similar in dissimilar communities. Urban, suburban, and rural communities find more commonality than difference in the types of concerns facing boards.

Priority Functions of Boards

Boards may have many duties and responsibilities, but boards generally have three major functions: (a) oversight and policy, (b) employment and supervision of top management, and (c) representation of the public constituency and clientele. These are the primary tasks for which an educational organization needs a functioning board, and they are instrumental in determining the informational needs of board members.

Oversight and Policy

In oversight and policy, any school system needs a body to conduct close and continuous analyses of organizational needs and direction. Well-intentioned people, without bias or vested interest, must deliberate with the public, top management, and their peers to set goals, to monitor organizational performance, and to make sure the system succeeds in accomplishing its pur-

1. Lack of financial support for schools
2. Declining student enrollment
3. Collective bargaining
4. Lack of parent interest
5. Ineffective management and leadership
6. Scarcity of "good" teachers
7. Substance abuse among youth

Exhibit 1.3. Top Issues and Concerns of Board Members

pose. Without such a body, the school system is helpless to control itself rationally.

The board is a critical part of the school system's health and operational well-being. It must look critically at planning, at leadership, and at performance. Moreover, the board not only serves in monitoring organizational outcomes and functioning but it serves in a judicial capacity as well. The policy role of the board is fundamental to the American school, and by institutionalizing its expectations in policy it serves its function appropriately. How the board fulfills its policy and oversight responsibilities has much, if not everything, to do with the quality of the schools.

Employment and Supervision of Top Management

The governing board must assure that its executive officer and staff are competent and performing in accordance with standards of the organization. Relationships with top management are critical to the success of the implementation and effectuation of board or system policy. Unless boards build into their operations and responsibilities the monitoring and nurturance of top management leadership, their efforts to support quality in the system may be thwarted. However, boards often confuse monitoring of executive functioning with prescribing "how" to get things done, or which things to do first. This provides a stultifying and confusing process of governance.

When the board steps down from its function of establishing expectations and values for the system through policy and begins to try to do the "work" in carrying out organizational expectations, the line between governance and management becomes blurred. When organizational relationships are confused, school operations are handicapped with counterproductive activity. This is true even if the board contains individuals who are available full- or nearly full-time, who have expertise in school operations, or who have experience in administering schools. The board's job is to govern, not to manage. As one veteran school board member, a highly successful businessman with over 40 years of board service in a large community, once said, "You don't need a dog if you're going to do your own barking." Do not neglect the power of governance through delegation.

A board must be free of operational responsibilities so that it can fulfill its own job—accountability for the organization's success or failure. Freedom from management details gives the board a better chance to monitor the complexities and particulars of school management. Motivation and compensation of people is also a requisite for quality institutional accomplishment. How the system rewards performance and excellence contributes to the achievement of the purposes and goals set by the board.

Representation of the Public Constituency

As board members quickly learn, they are elected officials with all of the incumbent rights, responsibilities, and *distresses* attendant thereto. School boards are closer to the electorate than any other form of volunteer-based government, and as a result they hear much, are expected to do much, and too often are rewarded little. Public involvement in education is characteristically American, offering the vibrancy and power of the people and the determination of direction by and for the people. Despite low voter turnout for school board elections, the public seems unwilling to abandon the local nature of school governance. A responsible board serves as an organ of consultation, communication, and decision making for all the people. Representation must be for no individual or group bias, but it must be aimed at the basic long-term interests of the system and the community it serves. Modern school systems have a multiplicity of constituencies and cultures. Parents are one constituency (or "customer") but are no longer the "owners" as the numbers of families with schoolchildren have dwindled. Parents, of course, are the consumers or providers of "clients" for the schools, and the needs of their children should drive the concerns, policies, and plans of the conscientious board.

Primarily, the board is the body by which the various publics are heard and served. With this public responsibility, boards and top management need to listen to what the diverse segments of the community want, to provide what they need to know, and to facilitate support for the educational system. School boards can provide a structure for the community to influence the vital policy issues facing schools, but sadly, they often do not do so (Twentieth Century Fund Task Force, 1992).

What Is at Stake for Board Members

The typical board member in America is atypical. That is, despite the complex and diverse cultural, ethnic, and human pluralistic nature of the American society, board members are unique. They are mostly male, their average age is in the midforties, they are most often white and married, they are highly educated themselves, and they are generally financially established and affluent as shown in Exhibits 1.4, 1.5, and 1.6 (Peirce, 1986).

The above exhibits illustrate that 64% of board members are male, 93% of board members are of the white race, and 57% of board members make more than $40,000 per year. Board members are also usually employed in professional or managerial jobs paying nearly twice the average salary nationally. They are successful. They are also relatively inexperienced in board service. The average board member is *in his or her first term*. This novice status could jeopardize the school system if there were no ways for board members to effectively learn the ramifications and procedural preferences of their job quickly. Without training and without information about issues, problems, and options, board members could easily be directing school systems from a position of ignorance

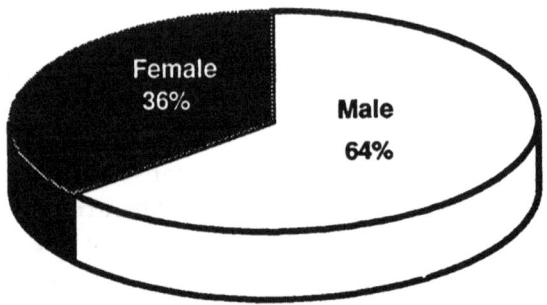

Exhibit 1.4. Board Member Characteristics: Gender

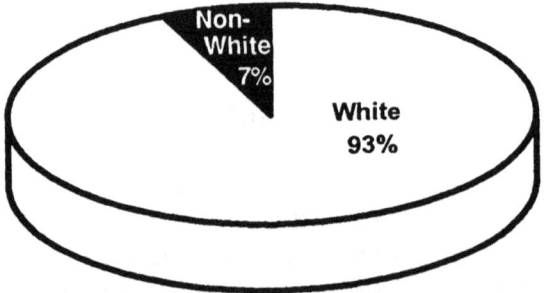

Exhibit 1.5. Board Member Characteristics: Race

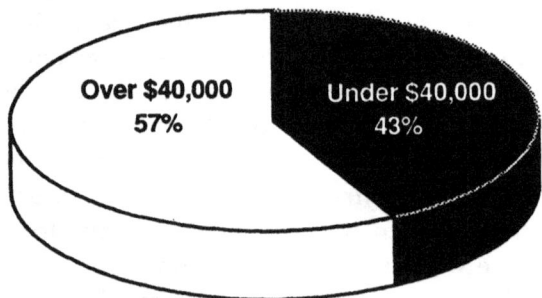

Exhibit 1.6. Board Characteristics: Annual Income

- Partnerships between schools, parents, teachers, and community leaders
- Increased academic expectations
- Improved supervision, training, and monitoring
- Focus on achievement and results
- Increased use of available time
- Enhanced safety and orderliness
- Increased faculty cohesion and collaboration
- Use of assessment feedback in instructional decisions

Exhibit 1.7. Initiatives for School Reform

and inexperience. Board members generally acknowledge that they lack preparation for board service, and many state that initially they were ignorant of the extensive knowledge and skills required of them. As mentioned earlier, improved decision making is facilitated and enhanced with adequate and appropriate information. Given proper preparation for the job, school board members, by virtue of their own success and capabilities, could be a real force for substantive and beneficial change in schools, and perhaps none too soon.

Messages from school reform from the past 10 years cry out for new initiatives and solutions (Manatt, 1992). Some of these initiatives are listed in Exhibit 1.7.

This is not the time to be timid or fuzzy-minded about changing the educational system. There is a growing sense of frustration about our schools, and boards are in a key position to take action to remedy or fix the problems of schooling. Given adequate and appropriate information and direction, proper decisions can be made, sound policies can be formulated, effective managerial action can be fostered, and results and performance can be monitored. That is precisely what is at stake—adequate and sound quality in school operations.

Board Processes for Change

Of course, it is not enough to simply call for change in school governance. The need is only foundational to change. "What is" is not good enough—"what ought to be" is both difficult to envision and to achieve. But if the current state of affairs in education is not good enough, then something else is called for. Doing what has always been done probably will not yield new results. More likely, doing what has always been done will produce what has always been achieved. The process of change connects all components of the school organization with people. Schools can change, but only if the people involved in their development and functioning change. Perceptions, ideas, and behaviors must be changed in the people of the organization with both internal and external relationships.

Premises for Change for Improvement of School System Quality

Several premises, or elements, are incorporated into appropriate change in school organizations. These elements are discussed below.

Change Is a Permanent Condition

Schools are dynamic organizations. Schools that have been successful over time have acknowledged that renewal and improvement are ongoing processes. The axiom of biology that says, "The difference in living and dead creatures is found in whether or not the creature is growing," is true in organizations as well. If an organization, or specifically a school system in this case, is not growing or improving more or less continually, it is dying or even dead. Organizations that continue to survive and succeed are improving themselves constantly. They meet new challenges, adapt to different conditions, incorporate innovation, and alter their programs and services to meet new and emerging needs. Without this commitment to ongoing development, the school system initially slows down, stultifies and becomes dull, and eventually suffers organizational "hardening of the arteries."

Board Values Direct Change

The school board is elected by the people to represent their interests. The beliefs, values, and vision of the community for their schools are placed in boards' hands with trust that the board will share and embed these values in institutional behavior. Board values influence change, and so do the values of everyone involved in the system. The challenge is to develop shared values and a covenant of common purpose for the school organization. In effect, the board communicates its vision to the people in the organization in order to get unity of purpose. As the board works with the human components of the system and the more unity of purpose is achieved, the more likely it is that positive change will occur. Everyone in the organization should have a clear understanding of and faith in what the school system stands for and where it is heading. This key element rests at the governance level, and boards must consider it to be a most serious and important responsibility.

Effective Organizational Vision Is Board Initiated

As corporate leaders, effective school board members share their clearly defined core values and expectations for the organization. The people who work in schools know what the values are and see them as the foundation of the climate and culture of the system. Broad consensus is pervasive throughout the system on what the focus of the system is, and everything that happens in the system is measured against that focus. Effective organizational vision is characterized by broad understanding and acceptance of direction, and the specifics of direction are widely known and followed. Of course, any vision must be worth the effort, and it must be congruent with the core values of the system. In quality terms, vision is the answer to the question, What is it that we are trying to accomplish? Given clear and unequivocal understanding and commitment to the organization's vision, the organization gains a better chance or advantage in achieving its goals.

Organizational Structures Are Means, Not Ends

Occasionally, organizational structures become institutionalized as things that exist and cannot be changed. However, no organizational configuration should be above evaluation for efficacy. In other words, Does it work? Or, more relevant to schools, Does it foster or advance learning? Sometimes, strategies and methods get treated like they are the goal, rather than part of a process to reach a goal. For example, ability grouping patterns, schedules, athletics and activities, grading, promotion and retention, demographic distributions, and punitive measures have become "sacred cows" and are accepted as givens. However, perpetual scrutiny of how well the organization is doing and how well the particular method in question affects the organization's performance is necessary in a healthy and improving system. Accepting the status quo simply because it is the status quo may be delimiting the organization's overall effectiveness and productivity. Comfort with things as they are may cause the organization to stand still and lose momentum for improvement. All organizational configurations should produce results, and those that do not should be modified. Simple solutions and program "bandwagons" require examination to ascertain their worth. Without commitment to continual assessment for improvement, no organization could ever hope to succeed in the long run.

Summary

Board members are in a unique position. They hold the key to many significant problems facing schools today, and they have control over priority functions that influence dramatically the quality of public schools more than any other organizational component. System oversight, leadership empowerment, and public representation are major responsibilities, and new initiatives are called for to improve the eroding level of quality among public schools. Change is needed, and board members must be equipped with tools and strategies to conquer whatever the future holds for public education.

Key Terms and Concepts

Governance. Implementation of legally authorized collective actions, functions, and decision-making powers of school boards.

Management. The supervisory and administrative personnel and functions of the organization, normally delegated by the governing board.

Vision. Collective expressions of values, expectations, and organizational purposes clearly understood and incorporated into operations and actions of the school organization.

References

Carver, J. (1991). *Boards that make a difference: A new design for leadership in nonprofit and public organizations.* San Francisco: Jossey-Bass.

Drucker, P. F. (1985). *Management: Tasks, responsibilities, practices.* New York: Harper & Row.

Galagan, P. A. (1988). Joining forces: Business and education take on competition. *Training and Development Journal, 42*(27), 26-29.

Goens, G. A., & Clover, S. I. R. (1992, October). Transforming schools: For real reform, you need to go beyond restructuring. *American School Board Journal, 179*(10), 41-42.

Institute for Educational Leadership. (1986). *School boards: Strengthening grass roots leadership.* Washington, DC: Author.

Leone, R. C. (1992). Foreword. In *Report of the Twentieth Century Fund Task Force on school governance.* New York: Twentieth Century Fund.

Manatt, R. P. (1992). *Vertical team training handbook.* Ames: Iowa State University, School Improvement Project.

Merl, J. (1990, March 28). Corporations find no easy education cure. *Los Angeles Times,* p. A3.

Peirce, N. R. (1986). Preface. In *School boards: Strengthening grass roots leadership.* Washington, DC: Institute for Educational Leadership.

Twentieth Century Fund Task Force. (1992). *Facing the challenge: The report of the Twentieth Century Fund Task Force on school governance.* New York: Twentieth Century Fund.

Williams, S. A. (1990). *Results from stratified random sample of public school superintendents on issues and suggestions for Center for Evaluation, Development and Research's proposed school board members' research handbook.* (Unpublished report). Bloomington, IN: Phi Delta Kappa International, Center for Development, Evaluation, and Research.

❖ 2 ❖

Applying Quality Principles
to Board Governance

School boards have the major responsibility for quality in a school system, and quality is never accidental. Quality in schooling is always the result of high intention, sincere effort, intelligent direction, and skillful execution. It represents a wise choice from among many alternatives (Foster, 1989). To participate in improving educational systems, boards must understand and follow certain principles. With the need for improvement established in the preceding chapter, it is now time to turn to what and how improvements can be made in an educational system.

Total Quality Education is within the grasp of any school board willing to explore ideas, concepts, techniques, and processes that are central to its creation and nurture. Total Quality Education means that a school system as a whole seeks and makes permanent an environment where all stakeholders and employees work to continually improve the quality of services provided to meet the needs of the customers or clientele of the system. The purpose of this chapter is to present the ideas and precepts of Total Quality Education with a flavor relevant to boards and governance functions. The processes and concepts of total quality improvement have been in existence for over 50 years, but they have not been seriously advocated for education until the past decade or so. After reading this chapter, board members should have a clear focus on what Total Quality Education is, how it works, and what the task of the board is in bringing it to reality within their own school system.

The Concept of Quality

Quality improvement in the United States was originally brought into focus by W. Edwards Deming, who had developed a set of procedures for continual improvement of processes in industry and manufacturing (Deming, 1982). Many of Deming's ideas were shunned by the captains of American industry, but they were enthusiastically embraced by the Japanese shortly after World War II. As many who are old enough will remember, Japanese products in the early postwar years were perceived as shoddy and cheaply made. No one with rational integrity would say that about Japanese products today. Japanese goods are widely perceived as being of very high quality, and Japanese companies as a rule delight their customers around the world with the value and dependability of their products. In gratitude for Deming's help in their reconstruction, the emperor of Japan conferred the Second Order Medal of the Sacred Treasure on him in 1960. The rest, of course, is history.

Deming's ideas often are characterized by a listing of the 14 points he enumerated in his book *Out of the Crisis* (Deming, 1986), and these are described later in this chapter. However, taken as a whole, Deming's ideas comprise a new philosophy and set of organizational values. The Deming philosophy deals with the importance of the customer, the criticality of design and planning in organizational behavior, the significance of consistency of performance compared to design, and the control of quality and its improvement over time. Quality improvement, or in this case Total Quality Education, is a new way of thinking and behaving for any organization. Quality improvement is no quick fix. Total Quality Education is a complex, deliberate, and focused process system that involves long-term commitment, patient implementation, continual development, and collaborative effort.

Definition of Quality

The word *quality* could mean different things to different people, especially in different contexts. However, in Total Quality Education, quality has a distinct and specific meaning. In its simplest terms, it means any of the features or basic characteristics that make something what it is; for example, a quality of schools is that students are generally found in them. In the context of existence, quality also refers to the degree of excellence that a thing or circumstance contains, or how good it may be.

In Total Quality Education, quality is defined by the client. For the Ford Motor Company, quality means "products and services that meet customers' needs and expectations at a cost that represents value" (Scherkenbach, 1991, p. 161). Quality also has durability. Meeting the customer's needs may not be enough. Suppose that a student's needs are met, and the student is satisfied with educational programs and services. Has the school organization provided quality? Not if the future success of the student is considered. Quality must meet and exceed the needs and the requirements of the client or customer, both present and future (Deming, 1982). In education, long-term consequences accrue to the client years, even decades, after receiving the services and programs of schools.

Quality in Total Quality Education begins with the intent of the governing board, resulting in client satisfaction and success. If the programs and services of the school organization not only meet but exceed the needs of the schools' clientele, both now and in the future, within a reasonable expenditure of resources, quality may be said to exist.

The words *total quality* expand the target to include a commitment to quality throughout all organizational efforts and activities and to a process to improve quality continually over the life of the organization. Total quality is a unifying principle that underlies all planning, actions, programs, and personnel in the organization, in which unequivocal fidelity for continuous improvement in everything is demonstrated. The Japanese call this fidelity or commitment to improvement *kaizen*.

The Deming Philosophy

Describing in detail what Deming calls "profound knowledge" is not within the scope of this book, but the key elements of the Deming philosophy are important enough to be introduced. When

Deming talks about the "new philosophy," he is talking about moving from quantitative thinking to qualitative thinking, from competition to cooperation, and from results at any cost to improvement of processes. Profound knowledge is characterized by dependency on theory, knowledge of variation, and predictability of future consequences from any configuration of information. The four parts of the Deming philosophy include (a) understanding of the concepts of a system, (b) theory of variation and use of statistical tools, (c) theory of knowledge, and (d) theory of psychology (Deming, 1990).

CONCEPT OF SYSTEM

For board members, the philosophical concept of "system" is an important one. Systems are complicated, intricate organizations composed of people and resources, working interdependently toward common ends. Each part of the system is dependent on the other parts, not unlike the many instruments in a large orchestra. When the instruments are working together properly, harmonious melodies result. When they are not working together, cacophony of sound (or clamor) results. A school district or corporation is a complex organism and consists of many parts. When all parts of the system are working together effectively, the system is likely to be successful. Optimization of all components in the system works to achieve higher levels of organizational functioning. The challenge for a board is to get the system working in harmony for maximum productivity.

THEORY OF VARIATION

Understanding variation is key to understanding total quality education. Variation simply refers to the range of difference that exists in any set of data. Data on any aspect of organizational performance are going to be varied; that is, they are going to be diverse and show some degree of dispersion. There are ways to measure central tendencies, such as computing the average of test scores for a group of students. However, the average or mean of any set of data does not show the range of response. Neither does the mean show whether dispersion in the data is due to a special or common cause.

Common causes are those forces affecting variation in measures of performance that are prevalent in the system itself. For example, test data from any group of students are going to reflect considerable variability that is ordinary in any randomly selected group. However, special causes of variation are attributable to some individual or identifiable force or problem in the system that might be correctable or influenced by an organizational action. For example, suppose that test results show that 20 fifth-grade classrooms in a school district cluster within a band not too far from the mean or average. Also suppose that one classroom's test results are noted to be far different and located way out of the band of scores for other classrooms. On closer inspection, one would probably find that the unusual classroom had some special problem or characteristics (i.e., incompetent teacher, no textbooks, unusually high percentages of "at-risk" students, etc.). The special causes might be minimized given some organizational intervention in a classroom, whereas common causes are pervasive through the entire system and require that the organization change overall.

It is critical that boards know the difference between common and special causes. Failure to differentiate might result in misdiagnosis of why the system is behaving one way and not another.

THEORY OF KNOWLEDGE

Knowledge is discovered or developed over time by careful interpretation of information based on empirical procedures and processes. Conditions, behaviors, and performance are measured and monitored to predict conclusions or outcomes in a consistent manner. For school boards, the theory of knowledge raises the ante in the game of deciding what courses of action are best for the system. How can the board know what course of action is better than all others, unless it has reliable, valid information based on research or past experiences? In decision making, careful attention must be paid to the amount, source, and verifiability of information. No board can have too much information in making decisions, and quality embodies knowledge applicable to all segments and actions of the school system. Statistical probability of results is valuable and helpful to boards in determining courses of action to follow for the organization.

Total Quality Education demands use of knowledge throughout the system. Sound organizational management focuses on the
expectations and mission of the school system; designs organizational behaviors and services accordingly; and uses accurate,
measured performance over time to judge how well the system is
achieving its goals. It is a continual and ongoing process. Two
questions should be useful to board members in this area: (a)
What is it we want to accomplish (goal/vision)? and (b) How will
we know whether or not we are doing a good job (assessment)?

THEORY OF PSYCHOLOGY

Only two things are needed to make an organization: people
and an activity or task. People are central to any organization and,
according to Deming's ideas, vice versa. Quality results from the
interaction of the people and the organization's systems. Just as
board members function best when they are well-informed, the
vast majority of problems will be prevented and improvement
will be fostered when people understand where they fit in and
when they have the knowledge they need to maximize their con-
tribution to the whole. The responsibility for the interdependent
relationships among people and processes rests with the governing board and its management team, led by the superintendent.

In the psychology of school organizations, it is important to
note that people are driven by intrinsic motives more than external stimuli, people seek relationships imbued with mutual respect
and self-esteem, and people are different in various ways but all
should cooperate as a team in improving the process (Tveite,
1989). In addition, fear must be driven out of an organization for
people to operate effectively, according to Deming. Fear inhibits
cooperation, stifles contributions, and removes incentive for development and improvement.

In a school system that uses the "new psychology," the following behaviors should be noted or observed:

- High levels of teamwork and cooperation
- People going out of their way to solve problems
- A willingness to experiment and try new ways of operating
- A commitment to doing the best job possible

If people are given respect and the authority to make decisions on issues that affect them, and if they feel as though they are a part of the system in general so that there is a sense of ownership for performance, the theory of psychology is at work in a positive way.

Measures and Criteria for Total Quality Education: The 14 Points

School boards, who conclude that quality of the system is critically important, need further direction as to what is expected of them. The "14 points" of quality organizational functioning (Deming, 1986) provide the guidance needed to implement the new philosophy in Total Quality Education. As these points are applied in the context of a school system, the intent of the precepts of total quality education can be preserved. One guiding principle will help in this approach. In Total Quality Education, the school board should focus on improvement of processes for the future and over the long haul rather than on immediate decisions for changes based on short-term, current results.

The 14 points will be enumerated by number as they appear in Deming's text, but perhaps they are better understood if grouped into five areas of common characteristics (Tveite, 1989), including the following:

- Purpose
- Leadership
- Collaborative effort
- Training and development
- Process improvement

In each of these categories, the 14 points for board members to use in Total Quality Education will be categorized into factors to initiate and factors to eliminate.

Purpose

The first of Deming's 14 points is, "Create constancy of purpose toward improvement of product and service, with the aim to become competitive and to stay in business, and to provide jobs" (Deming, 1982, pp. 23-24). The question board members should ask is, What does American society need from our schools? Answers to that question will give strong clues as to the ways in which school systems can provide services that are congruent with society's most fundamental needs. Specifically, the aim should be toward improvement of learning and services that enable and empower learners to improve all forms of processes and to enter meaningful positions in society.

With constancy of purpose, the board establishes services and processes to meet the needs of the system's clientele, both now and into the future. Management is charged with the responsibility to continually improve the organization's functioning and delivery of services. When there is constancy of purpose, an environment exists where there is a powerful, shared vision of what the organization's purpose is and how it can be carried out. The organization is going to be characterized by efforts to move in a single direction, with congruency of effort, and over a long-term period of time. In short, values drive change. Real change is grounded in the values, beliefs, and principles of the people of the organization. Real improvement rests on a covenant of shared ideas and purpose (Goens & Clover, 1992).

The 14th point in Deming's list says, "Put everyone in the company to work to accomplish the transformation" (Deming, 1982, pp. 23-24). Everyone in the school system, from the learners to the board, has something valuable to contribute to improvement in the system. Empowering the organization's people to work together in concert recognizes that the people closest to the work are the most knowledgeable about it. Also, all resources of the organization are used in accomplishing needed changes. An organization is more than a sum of its separate parts. The important changes must occur in how the school system's people think and behave. Given involvement of all parties concerned with the system, a synergistic effect results, building a stronger and stronger focus for improvement.

Leadership

In this category, one point calls for establishment or initiation of a new action, and three points call for elimination of existing

- Understand how the work of their group fits into the overall purposes of the system.
- Create for everyone joy in work.
- Optimize the skills, training, and abilities of everyone, and help them to improve.
- Use information to help them understand their people and themselves, understand variation, and use statistical calculation to identify and work on special causes or problems.
- Create trust, listen, and learn.

Exhibit 2.1. Leader Behaviors in Quality Improvement Processes

actions. Deming's (1982) Point 7 states, "Initiate leadership. The aim of leadership should be to help people and equipment and gadgets to do a better job." (pp. 23-24). Leadership in schools consists of removing the barriers for improving processes. Anything that gets in the way of the workers taking pride in their work is a barrier, and leaders must work to remove all barriers. This cannot be done by carrot-and-stick rewards or punitive arrangements. Rather, the leader becomes coach and mentor in working with teachers, parents, staff, learners, and members of the community to improve all processes and environments in the system to value and encourage learner growth and improvement. In Total Quality Education, leading is helping. Deming (1986) characterized leaders and leader attributes as shown in Exhibit 2.1

On the other hand, Deming cites three points calling for elimination of judgmental behavior on the part of leadership. Point 11 says, "Eliminate work standards and quotas. Eliminate management by objective. Eliminate management by numbers, numerical goals. Substitute leadership" (Deming, 1982, pp. 23-24). Rather than looking at how many times the target is hit, it is better to work on improving the factors that affect the accuracy that results in hits or misses of the target. In management by objective, the objective becomes the goal, rather than the process, and suboptimization may result. For example, in a cost-saving proposal, one component of the system might benefit but only at the

expense of another. Perhaps transportation costs could be reduced, but school schedules might be compressed, causing incon-
venience for learners. Perhaps costs of procurement could be
reduced, causing teachers to dig into their own pockets for teaching
materials.

Point 12 states, "Remove barriers that rob people of their right
to pride of work. This means abolishment of the annual or merit
rating and of management by objective, management by the numbers" (Deming, 1982, pp. 23-24). This point is often misunderstood.
A good organization uses information for feedback, employees are
entrusted with feedback information, and problems are pointed
out as they occur. However, performance appraisal is established
to focus on improvement of processes, and judgment of results is
eliminated in terms of ranking and rating of people.

Fear is the natural by-product in competitive rating and ranking systems. Fear of failure and fear of making errors can strangle
innovation and creativity. This underscores Point 8, "Drive out
fear, so that everyone may work effectively for the company"
(Deming, 1982, pp. 23-24). Workers become fearful when management sets targets and rewards or punishes those who reach or fall
short of the target. The same can be said for learners when it
comes to grades. We know from research that grades do not moti-
vate; rather, grades undermine the intrinsic joy of learning and
become ends in themselves, thwarting learning. Fear is counterproductive to school systems and it is destructive of a positive
culture. Power, responsibility, and rewards must be shared widely
to eliminate fear, and the environment must be such that all parties feel comfortable contributing to the improvement efforts.

Collaborative Effort

Three points are included in this area, two calling for action
eliminating current practices and one calling for action establishing a new practice. Point 9 states, "Break down barriers between departments," and Point 4 states, "End the practice of
awarding business on the basis of price alone." New practice is
requested with Point 2, "Adopt a new philosophy" (Deming,
1982, pp. 23-24). Basically, Deming is talking about the conse-

quences of economic competition and focusing on costs rather than on the overriding purpose of the school system or company.

In the case of breaking down barriers, teacher and learner productivity is enhanced when departments combine talents to create more congruent opportunities for system improvement. In the school context, articulation up and down the system will produce greater vertical consistency, and coordination and cooperation across grade levels and content areas will produce greater horizontal consistency. In both cases, greater likelihood of meeting the customer's (or client's) needs will occur. Point 4 on price tag alone must be taken in the context of supplier and customer. In the school system, the school and the community fulfill this context. Recognizing and honoring commitment to Total Quality Education means that, through trust and cooperation between the community and its school system, improvement will be fostered with emphasis on efficiency and productivity, rather than simple price tag (or taxpayer cost). Given understanding and appreciation of what is provided for a specific amount of money, support from taxpayers of a school system for the additional cost is generally obtained.

The new philosophy Deming calls for has been explained above, but the new philosophy would be recognized by quality focus, cooperation in relationships, customer satisfaction priority, and win-win processes. In the win-win context, if anyone in the system wins at the expense of any other, then everyone loses. It is better for all to cooperate and gain or win. For example, the adversarial negotiations between teachers' unions and school boards cause everyone to lose, even if someone wins. Productivity overall is diminished in proportion to the time and energy devoted to the process of negotiating for advantage by either or both sides. The time-worn slogan, "Together Everyone Accomplishes More," (or TEAM) underscores this point.

Training and Development

There is no substitute for training and professional growth in a school system. In fact, there is no substitute for training and professional growth for school board members as well as for all other members of the educational team. The board must establish the structure and framework that provides ongoing and perpetual training for all participants in the system in order to better determine the client's needs and to meet those needs accordingly. In Point 6, the precept is, "Institute training on the job." Point 13 says, "Institute a vigorous program of education and self-improvement" (Deming, 1982, pp. 23-24).

Whereas Point 6 focuses on training in skills and knowledge related to specific jobs or tasks, Point 13 calls for education of the workforce in innovation and opportunities for improvement. Training programs for the job should have the objectives of helping each worker perform the specifics of the job better, understand how his or her job fits into the overall whole of the system's purposes, and develop skill in carrying out the work. Three major components would be found in effectively delivering these factors. These three components include evidence that workers (a) have the capability to set goals, (b) demonstrate ways and means to work more effectively, and (c) are able to assess the quality of their own work.

In Point 13, everyone in the system would be provided continuous learning programs to get and keep the school system on the cutting edge and to enhance clientele satisfaction. Exploring ideas and broad interests beyond the boundaries of the specific job would benefit administrators, teachers, support staff, board members, and others on the educational team in terms of helping the system improve over time.

Process Improvement

If a school board implements Total Quality Education, it would turn away from dependence on inspection and reliance on unreliable measures of performance. Point 3 requires the school system to "cease dependence on inspection to achieve quality" (Deming, 1982, pp. 23-24). This point has special relevance for educational systems because it refers to end-of-the-line judgment of system results, rather than benchmarks along the way. It is an expensive and ineffective way to get quality and simply will not work in the context of schooling. By the time the client or learner completes his or her schooling, it is too late to decide whether or not the results are satisfactory.

A better process to improve quality is to use diagnostic and prescriptive instruments throughout the learning process, especially how well the learner can apply information and skills to real-life situations. Moreover, learners need to know how to measure their own progress and quality of their work if they are to take ownership of their own learning and development. For teachers, assessment information should provide guidance for self-improvement and enhancement of performance in learner progress and accomplishment. Annual, standardized tests are inadequate for this purpose. Better forms of assessment for improving teaching and learning are discussed further in chapter 6.

Point 10 states, "Eliminate slogans, exhortations, and targets for the work force asking for zero defects and new levels of productivity" (Deming, 1982, pp. 23-24).

Artificial manipulations in motivation are no substitute for sound preventative actions in system management. Slogans and such designed to "inspire" and "challenge" workers are not likely to get people to work better or harder. In fact, this process is grounded on a flawed premise—that the workers are responsible for the results. Perhaps they are or are not, but slogans and exhortations seem to attempt to fix blame on individuals, rather than on a system. Perhaps slogans can emerge from the system team voluntarily, and they could actually contribute to pride and joy in work given equitable distribution of power, responsibility, and rewards. In essence, exhortations and slogans may foster adversarial relationships and undermine cooperative effort.

Point 5 calls for improvement of process: "Improve constantly and forever the system of production and service, to improve quality and productivity, and thus constantly decrease costs" (Deming, 1982, pp. 23-24). Eliminating bad results should be the focus of the entire system and of all its participants. A major responsibility is found here for the governing board: empowering the educational team through the superintendent of schools to make continuous progress in product and service improvement,

- A pervasive belief structure that places intense, empirical priority on client needs
- A sense of ownership in the services delivered by the school system among all organizational members
- A shared, commonly held sense of purpose and vision of the organization's mission
- Supported commitment to innovation, and elimination of barriers to improvement in all levels of the organization
- The feeling of interdependence—that everyone is in the organization's work together—and commitment to the common and greater good

Exhibit 2.2. Organizational Attributes of Total Quality Education

to minimize waste and inefficiency, and to help teachers and staff improve the quality of their learning and other aspects of professional development.

Total Quality Education is the product of focused effort to make the system's processes congruent with customer needs. The governing board has the most significant role to play. The board must purposely put in place ways and means to foster the organizational attributes outlined in Exhibit 2.2.

The school board probably holds 85% of the system's potential for quality improvement. Given the need for direction from the top in terms of commitment to Total Quality Education, the board should direct efforts to make the system's design congruent with customer needs.

THE PDCA CYCLE

Implementation of this process might be best achieved with use of a continuous, ongoing improvement of every process. One of the best ways is to use the "Shewhart-Deming Improvement Cycle" (Deming, 1986). This cycle is implemented through a "plan-do-check-act" (PDCA) process, as illustrated in Exhibit 2.3.

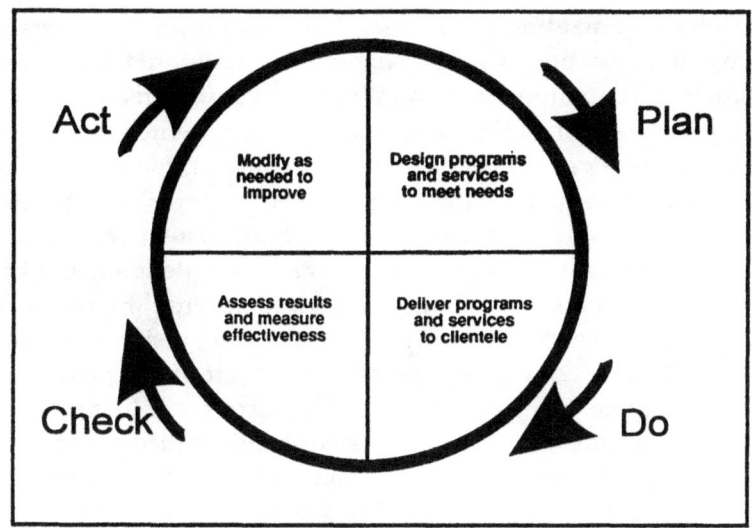

Exhibit 2.3. The Shewhart-Deming (PDCA) Cycle

The PDCA cycle is useful in continuing Total Quality Education. For example, a new course could be planned and developed, implemented, assessed, and modified as needed to manifest improvement in a specific program. All programs and services would be subjected to an ongoing analysis of their effectiveness for continual improvement. Ideally, this process transcends the entire system, with all components and processes working together in harmony to effect improvement.

In this context, board members would expect that schools would change dramatically, albeit gradually, over time. Some have commented that schools of today are not much different than schools of a couple of decades ago, and with continual improvement, this could not be the case.

Board Expectations and Organizational Mission

Participants in the school system need a sense of direction. People need to know what the organization stands for, where it is headed, and what it is going to take to become better in terms of defined organizational purpose. A meaningful shared organizational purpose bonds people together in unity and incorporates them into a common direction. Without clear understanding of the aims of the organization, disparate and fragmented activities result. Progress cannot occur without a common focus on purpose and goals. The board is the body that has responsibility for determining the values upon which the school system rests, and the board must create, with the help of the superintendent and his or her educational team, a consensus view of what the purpose of schooling in their community must be. Again, vision is the key.

The local school board is acting in behalf of the people in its community to translate educational purposes into reality. The board envisions the community's educational future and formulates the goals, defines the outcomes, and sets the course for its public schools (National School Board Association, 1992).

Methods for Delivering Quality

Once the creation of a common belief and value structure for schooling has been facilitated, the board can proceed with defining plans, rules, relationships, and job descriptions that will move the system toward its vision. Clear expression of beliefs and values by the board is followed by active discussion and conversation about that vision with members of the community. The board should seek to inform the community about its set of values and defined purposes, and nurture commitment and support for them. Effective boards use this process to build a sense of community that brings factions and groups together in working toward common ends for the greater good of the community.

The board empowers its chief executive officer to develop and to implement strategies and procedures to help the district realize its mission. The board also evaluates and determines the worth of plans and procedures in terms of their relevance and effect on achievement of the district vision.

Successful implementation of Total Quality Education would demonstrate organizational evidence listed in Exhibit 2.4.

- A clear vision of what the system can and should become is expressed.
- Values projected by board members and organizational participants demonstrate a match between what is said and what is done.
- Concern for the needs and benefits of the organization's clientele is a primary focus, including the well-being of the internal "customers."
- Cooperation is evidenced across and throughout the system with clear coherent strategies for operations in place.
- Diagnosis of the organization's effectiveness is constant, and meaningful data are used for modification of practices and services on an ongoing basis.
- High levels of responsibility are correlated with high levels of innovation, with a desire to improve the status quo and teamwork.

Exhibit 2.4. Organizational Evidence of Total Quality Education

Total Quality Education school systems are characterized by a particular kind of governance behavior. Boards in great school systems have communicated very clearly to everyone in the organization that they are serious about continuous improvement and in making it work. They do this by being believable, unambiguous, consistent, and optimistic. Believability means the board values something deeply and it is projecting that conviction. Unambiguous means that the board has clearly thought through what quality means, and it has a convincing argument for its commitment that makes sense to the organizational members. Consistency means agreement and commitment to a rational course of action that is unwavering and steadfast in all situations. Optimism is characterized by confidence that Total Quality Education matters and it can and will happen in its school district.

Given these attributes, the governing board is not just giving lip service to quality enhancement in its schools, but is living evidence of commitment and support for Total Quality Education. Modeling such commitment is far more important than any other element of educational governance.

Summary

The purpose of this chapter was to present the concepts of Total Quality Education in the context of school board governance. The theory of profound knowledge includes understanding of variation, systems, people, and knowledge development. Deming's 14 points were presented in a format incorporating five dimensions of organizational functioning: purpose, leadership, collaborative effort, training and development, and continual improvement. The theory behind the 14 points holds that school boards should be focused on improvement of processes instead of judgment of results. In short, as W. Edwards Deming (1982) would say, "Don't fix blame, fix the system" (pp. 55, 118). If boards understand the theory undergirding total quality education, they can then interpret how to apply the principles to their school systems and to their governance responsibilities.

Key Terms and Concepts

Constancy of purpose. A pervasive and powerful shared vision of what the organization's chief aims are and a commitment to carry them out with congruency of effort over long periods of time.

Deming principles. The collection of ideas and precepts for organizational quality improvement embodied in the writings and teachings of W. Edwards Deming.

Kaizen. A Japanese term meaning "dedication to continuous improvement."

Knowledge. Comprehension of information and the act or state of knowing based on empirically developed processes and subject to independent verification consistently over time.

Leadership. The act and responsibility of removal of barriers that stand in the way of organizational improvement, joy in work, optimization of effort, and the creation of trust and mutual cooperation.

Quality. Any of the features or basic characteristics that make something what it is, and the degree of excellence, perfection, or amount of value that it represents or contains.

System. A complicated, intricate organization composed of many people and resources, working independently toward common ends.

Teamwork. The state or participatory interdependence characterized by mutual cooperation among all people involved in the organization's work, common commitment to organizational excellence, and a widespread feeling of joy without fear.

Total Quality Education. The character of a school system evidenced by a shared clear vision, concern for clientele, cooperation among all people, ongoing improvement efforts, and increased productivity over time.

Variation. The range of difference that exists in any set of data or information.

References

Deming, W. E. (1982). *Out of the crisis.* Cambridge: MIT Press.

Deming, W. E. (1986). *Out of the crisis.* Cambridge: MIT Center for Advanced Engineering Study.

Deming, W. E. (1990, July). *Foundation for management of quality in the Western world.* Paper presented at the meeting of the Institute of Management Sciences, Osaka, Japan. In *An introduction to total quality for schools* (1991). Alexandria, VA: American Association of School Administrators.

Foster, W. A. (1989). Foreword. In H. R. McAlindon, *Commitment to quality* (p. 5). Lombard, IL: Great Quotations.

Goens, G. A., & Clover, S. I. R. (1992). Transforming schools. *American School Board Journal, 179*(10), 41-42.

Ishikawa, K. (1985). *What is total quality control? The Japanese way.* Englewood Cliffs, NJ: Prentice-Hall.

National School Board Association. (1992). NSBA on the revitalized role of the school board. *The American School Board Journal, 179*(11), 29.

Scherkenbach, W. W. (1991). *Deming's road to continual improvement.* Knoxville, TN: SPC Press.

Tveite, M. D. (1989). The theory behind the fourteen points: Management focused on improvement instead of on judgment. In *An introduction to total quality for schools* (1991). Alexandria, VA: American Association of School Administrators.

✧ 3 ✧

Using Policy to Implement Board Vision

The future of public schools and of our society depends on the quality of board governance. In point of fact, no other body in American society has more power to effect change to maintain our country's preeminence in the world of tomorrow than does the local school board. Boards govern approximately 15,000 school districts, employ over 3 million people nationwide, oversee the expenditure of over $200 billion, and are in control of the educational opportunities for nearly 50 million students.

Given this magnitude of clout, boards undertake the single most important responsibility found in our culture. Thomas Jefferson alluded to this important responsibility when he said, "Those who want people to be ignorant and free expect something that never was and never will be." Education is the avenue toward a productive and meaningful life, and it is the foundation of our free society. It has kept this country free and remains a bulwark against subjugation of the minds and hearts of our widely diverse people. Maintaining the viability of educational institutions falls on the shoulders of governing boards.

Policy and Quality Processes and Precepts

The purpose of any organization is generally reflected in its policies and activities. In the Total Quality Education framework, policy is the means by which values, beliefs, and expectations of the community are translated by boards into a framework to guide operations and practices. Everyone in the organization needs a framework of theory and beliefs to direct experience and outcomes of the system (Melvin, 1991). The framework is policy. Fashioned from shared values, honed with knowledge of what works, and established in clear, unequivocal language, policy guides, directs, inspires, and informs everyone in the organization as to what the system aims or seeks to do. Without the framework, the organization is like a rudderless ship—it could go anywhere, even where it is not wanted or where it might self-destruct.

The central point of policy responsibility for governing boards is that rhetoric about goals and standards is meaningless unless the mechanism is put into place to achieve them (Holt, 1993). The principles of quality are discussed in the preceding chapter, but two key points emerge for consideration by board members.

Quality Is Defined by the Customer

Clearly, schools do not exist as ends in themselves, but for the benefit of those whom they serve (Harris & Bagget, 1992). The notion of customers may seem strange to school people, but it must never be forgotten that, if an institution fails to meet the needs of its customers or clientele, the institution will lose those customers to some other institution that meets those needs. This competitive notion was found in the push for school choice endorsed by the Reagan-Bush administration during the 1980s. Perhaps rightfully so, for if an institution, in this case a school system, gets smug or complacent about the job it is doing, the clients may suffer.

School clients depend on the board to anticipate their future needs. Because Deming finds customers everywhere (Scherkenbach, 1991), it is especially important for boards to decide just who they are really trying to serve. As "customers," their needs and future requirements are defined by the board. Boards must understand and improve the process to meet the needs of school clients or customers. In schools, the customer is most likely the student rather than the parent. The product is the school's curriculum provided to the student. Improvement of the product is gained by (a) attending to the instructional practices, (b) responding to future anticipated demands on students, and (c) monitoring the effectiveness of the curriculum with comprehensive forms of assessment, not just traditional tests.

Customer Focus

Quality improvement is not a linear process that, if followed, will result in higher quality. Design of programs and services must fit the needs of the clientele. The customer's needs must be the focus of the organization in all internal processes that deal with continuous improvement. What the system must do is use an organized process to identify and prioritize customer needs and then shape the organization's resources into aligning products and services to meet those priorities consistently. In effect, continuous improvement focused on the needs of the customer is one of the major functions of governance, and it may be achieved through policy design and implementation. A schematic showing the process of customer focus is depicted in Exhibit 3.1 (GOAL/QPC Research Committee, 1990).

In Total Quality Education, a school system provides structure for meeting and exceeding customer needs and expectations. However, without broad systemwide involvement in the planning and implementation of the quality improvement process, all levels of the organization cannot be focused on providing products and services that satisfy the customer or clientele demands. In the process, customer demands are identified and prioritized. Once the needs and demands are identified, and the relative importance of each is established, the board and superintendent move to align the school system's services and programs (products) with those needs. The voice of the customer is captured in a process that provides clarity of direction and an analysis of quality characteristics, costs, reliability, and new concepts and technologies for improvement. Information on customer needs is gathered by listening to the customer through research, analysis of complaints, surveys, longitudinal evaluations, and other means in the steps enumerated in Exhibit 3.2.

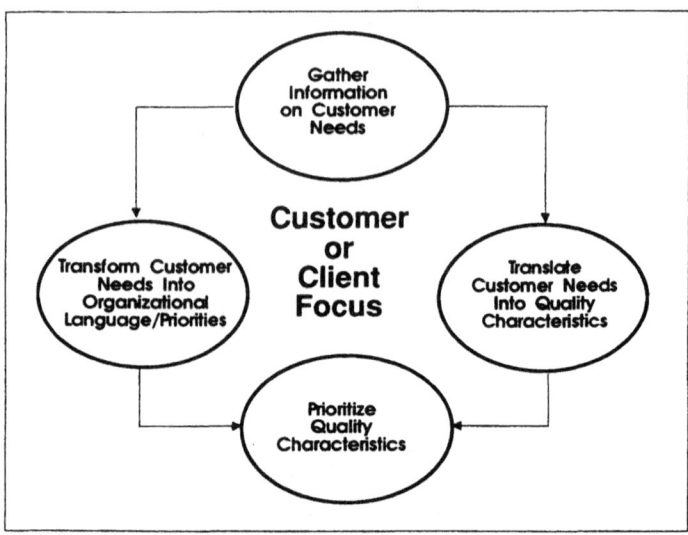

Exhibit 3.1. Sequence of Targets in Customer Focus

Translating customer needs into school system priorities involves (a) using and interpreting the data and the information gathered for determining the relative importance of customer needs, (b) determining how well those demands are being met, and (c) determining where in the system improvement is needed. The steps are suggested in Exhibit 3.3.

Interpreting prioritized customer needs in schools for service and program improvements calls for several steps as listed in Exhibit 3.4.

School boards may find the process affected by the voice of the organization as well as the voice of the customer or client. Resistance to change will always be present in any organization regardless of the perceived benefit of the change. This "voice" will need to be taken into account by the governing board. Data and tools must be used not only to assure appropriate organizational response to needs but to save the organization time and money as well. Focusing on customer needs is a continual, ongoing process.

1. Gather information from existing clientele and students.
2. Gather information from nonclientele (community, business, etc.).
3. Identify areas of need and potential for improved services or programs.
4. Organize customer demands into related groupings.

Exhibit 3.2. Steps in Gathering Customer Needs Information

1. Review and study the relative importance of customer needs and demands.
2. Determine the level of current satisfaction of needs by the system.
3. Identify the potential areas for quality improvement.
4. Determine the level or place in the system where change is required to meet needs.
5. Verify the authenticity of customer demands (assure that status quo is not influencing perceptions of the message from the customer).

Exhibit 3.3. Translating Customer Needs Into Priorities

1. Match customer needs and demands with components that relate to each demand.
2. Sort and group quality improvements that measurably affect or meet customer demands.
3. Set priorities of changes and improvements based on customer demand relevance.
4. Select or recommend means for improvement of products, services, and programs.

Exhibit 3.4. Interpreting Customer Needs Into Improvement

Quality Emanates From the Top

Quality is not an entity—it is a way of doing things. The board translates its expectations and values into action through policy and system oversight. Desirable states or desired conditions are translated into concrete statements of process. This becomes the mechanism for achieving standards and goals. In essence, the link between what the board thinks is important and the organization's practices is found in board-determined expectations established in writing and shared widely throughout the organization. This couples what is desired (theory) with what is delivered (practice).

Role of the Governing Board in Improvement

The governing board and top management must not only initiate total quality improvement but they must become directly involved in its formulation and implementation (Law, 1993). New ways of thinking and operating require more than noisy fanfare and catchy slogans. The commitment and involvement of those at the top of the organization serve as a model for people in the organization. Actions speak louder than words, and when people in the organization see the board and the superintendent spending the time and the effort necessary to make quality improvement processes work, its chances of success improve significantly.

Given these two precepts to consider in the context of policy, theory and practice come together through a problem-solving process undertaken by the board. In quality terms, school boards establish a professional culture with a shared vision, promote team collaboration in changing practices to better respond to the way both students and staff learn and progress, and build coherent and complex human activity in order to realize the valued goals of the organization. There is no more effective way of developing such a vision and empowering such an organization than through policy and delegated management, congruent with the client's needs.

Local boards are often mystified as to why state and federal policy makers are preempting the discretion of local boards (Twentieth Century Fund Task Force, 1992). However, where one

---

1. Determining critical products and services that fulfill the organization's mission and meet customer needs
2. Monitoring and measuring performance of the organization against its mission and customer needs
3. Reviewing and sharing information about performance, assuring to "drive out fear," and focusing organizational efforts toward improvement

---

Exhibit 3.5. Policy Functions of Boards in Quality Improvement

level of government does not act to meet the needs of its clientele, the natural progression of authority in such cases is to the next higher level of governance. If local school boards are perceived to fail to initiate reform or change in schools to better meet student needs, then state policy makers step in to solve the problem. To become recognized as competent and effective policy makers, local school boards must become proactive, initiating quality principles for institutional change through policy.

Policy Functions in Quality Improvement

Critical processes in building Total Quality Education begin with the board and cascade down through the organization. Customer needs provide the means to determine the key processes and activities of the organization, but customer needs also prescribe the mechanisms for monitoring the organization. Primarily, the board performs three policy functions, which are listed in Exhibit 3.5.

The board must be careful to use the process to provide knowledge about improvement needs, not to fix blame on individual or component performance. The task is to manage and actively use feedback information to focus the organization's resources on areas for improvement. Although resistance to measuring performance in critical processes is to be expected, knowledge about the system's performance is a powerful tool for ongoing improvement in achieving the organization's basic mission and strategic goals.

Policy Effectiveness and Benchmarking

Benchmarking is a useful quality development tool in industry, and it has applicability in Total Quality Education, especially governance, as well. Benchmarking is simply a procedure of ranking potentially useful new ideas for processes, actions, practices, methods, and policies in an orderly manner based on effectiveness demonstrated by other organizations (Bonstingl, 1992). Benchmarking assumes that the organization is constantly and regularly searching for new ways to improve, and it does not accept anything less than achieving the theoretical best from the organization. Good organizations know that they can and must get better. Poor organizations feel that the organization "isn't broken, and doesn't need fixing." However, given the 30% student dropout rate in American high schools, it seems foolish for any board to claim that their school system cannot get better in meeting the needs of their clientele.

Some keys for looking at the role and the performance of school boards based on principles of governance that might be used as benchmarks include the criteria (Carver, 1991a) shown in Exhibit 3.6.

Evidence indicates that boards spend too little time on education policy, policy oversight, leadership for public education, and systemic educational improvement (Twentieth Century Fund Task Force, 1992). Perhaps if a board uses benchmarking, including the key criteria delineated above, ongoing commitment to Total Quality Education can be achieved.

Summary

No institutional governance body has more clout than local school boards in fashioning quality in their systems. Within a system, the board sets the direction that should be based on the needs and the requirements of those who are served by education—clients and customers. Building a customer-focused organization calls for gathering information on customer needs, transforming needs into quality improvements, and setting priorities for action.

- Board accountability to the public for the totality of the performance, destiny, and behavior of the school system
- Board responsibility, as a body, to serve the general public rather than special interest groups, community subgroups, or employed professionals
- Board governance of the system without interference or involvement in management, which should be left to the administration
- Maintenance of focus of attention and occupation on clientele and students rather than involvement in detail of other responsibilities (fiscal, facilities, employer, etc.)
- Board obligation to define and clarify that for which the school system exists, in this case purposes, values, and expectations for the system, without embroilment or participation in how the ends are to be met beyond establishing the framework for Total Quality Education
- Board covenant to assess its ability and performance in governing the school system and to obtain whatever training, data, and knowledge are necessary to govern effectively

Exhibit 3.6. Benchmarks for Building Quality From the Top

Quality begins with the governing board. Failure of boards to grasp the challenge of improving quality often results in preemptive control from higher levels of government. To provide quality effectively, three policy functions are essential, and benchmarks for building quality are recommended.

Key Terms and Concepts

Benchmarking. A procedure of ranking ideas, processes, methods, and policies based on effectiveness demonstrated in other organizations used in determinations for improvement efforts.

Customer focus. A demonstrated commitment and thrust of the organization's people and resources toward meeting the needs and the requirements and enhancing the benefit of the client or those served by the organization.

References

Bonstingl, J. J. (1992). *Schools of quality: An introduction to total quality management in education.* Alexandria, VA: Association for Supervision and Curriculum Development.

Brodinsky, B. (1977). *How a school board operates.* Bloomington, IN: Phi Delta Kappa Educational Foundation.

Carver, J. (1991a). *Boards that make a difference.* San Francisco: Jossey-Bass.

Carver, J. (1991b). *Recommendations to the West Virginia Legislative Oversight Commission on Education Accountability.* Carmel, IN: Carver Governance Design.

Deming, W. E. (1982). *Out of the crisis.* Cambridge: MIT Press.

English, F. W. (1988). *Curriculum auditing.* Lancaster, PA: Technomic.

GOAL/QPC Research Committee. (1990). *Total quality management master plan: An implementation strategy.* Methuen, MA: GOAL/QPC.

Harris, J. W., & Baggett, J. M. (1992). *Quality quest in the academic process.* Birmingham, AL: Samford University Press.

Holt, M. (1993, January). The educational consequences of W. Edwards Deming. *Phi Delta Kappan,* pp. 382-388.

Law, J. E. (1993, June). Leaping over the pitfalls of TQM. *School Business Affairs,* pp. 21-23.

Melvin, C. A. (1991). Restructuring schools by applying Deming's management theories. *Journal of Staff Development, 12*(3), 16-20.

Scherkenbach, W. W. (1991). *Deming's road to continual improvement.* Knoxville, TN: SPC Press.

Twentieth Century Fund Task Force. (1992). *Facing the challenge: The report of the Twentieth Century Fund Task Force on School Governance.* New York: Twentieth Century Fund.

❖ 4 ❖

Designing Policy for
Quality Improvement

Effective boards are skilled makers, enforcers, and monitors of policy. It is virtually impossible to effectively govern a local school district, big or small, without a wide range of policies. Policies are needed for curriculum, instruction, personnel, employment, student relations, assessment, budgeting, fiscal management, administration, planning and direction, facilities, community relations, equity, and other areas of governance. In addition, policies guide the board itself in its own governance activities.

Policies are necessary for orderly management (Brodinsky, 1977). Policy design, delivery, and assessment are a big task, and it is perhaps the most important and effective way that a board can spend its time and energy.

What Is Often Wrong With Policy

Boards often find themselves overwhelmed with a flurry of events and activities. They spend a lot of hours dealing with multitudinous items brought to them by the public, the staff, and the administration. Cumbersome, voluminous policy manuals seem to hinder more than help, and most policies are prescriptive in detail and concern staff practices. Some policies are actually sanctions of administrative prerogatives, such as deciding school schedules, bus routes, or approving insignificant purchases. When this happens, it means that the administration has either shuffled the decision-making monkey off its back to the board, or the board has mistakenly assumed the administration's role.

Moreover, board policies often offer little clue as to what the board should do, and some policies are often self-contradictory, impotent, or meaningless. Many boards have noted that they have policies that are no longer relevant or followed, and some practices of the organization operate without or outside policy guidance. Such policies are dead but unburied in the first instance, and alive but invisible in the second instance.

How Policies Can Make a Difference

In Total Quality Education, constancy of purpose is essential. The essence of any organization lies in what it believes, what it stands for, and what and how it values (Carver, 1991a). Once the board conceptualizes the organization's purposes, the actions and decisions of the organization follow in turn based on the framework of values and perspectives. Total Quality Education begins by recognition of this important, primary characteristic of the school organization. Decisions of all types in the system rest, either by intention or default, on board-fashioned principles and universal organizational comprehension, both of which build congruence and consistency for the organization as a whole. A well-defined purpose or mission gives the organization a unifying force—something to build cooperation and mutually supportive team effort around. Recognized and properly applied, values and expectations stated in policy offer the organization keys to success and quality improvement.

Regrettably, most school systems neglect this important responsibility (Downey, 1993). In quality terms, the system fails to define the nature of its business or the properties of its products. Boards must provide a clear direction to the system for quality control (English, 1988). Policy provides a series of connecting links between purpose and mission, mission and vision, vision and programs, and so on. Rational, productive organizations have crystal-clear understandings of what the business is about and established policies to define direction for the organization.

- The board demonstrates it is running a businesslike organization.
- Board actions are given credibility and respect because of documentation and codification of intentions.
- Legal records are established and maintained.
- Stability and continuity are fostered regardless of board or staff changes; idiosyncrasy and political influences are minimized.
- The public has a means to evaluate board performance.
- Fair and consistent actions facilitate improvement of staff morale.
- Orientation of new board members and staff is provided and assisted.
- Appraisal, evaluation, and accountability are facilitated for board and staff.

Exhibit 4.1. Outcomes and Benefits of Written Policies

Reasons that written policies are important in a rational school system include the outcomes (National School Board Association, 1992) listed in Exhibit 4.1, resulting from properly drafted policies.

In addition to the reasons listed above, four additional reasons for developing and establishing written policies have been identified (Downey & Frase, in press). Written policies result in additional benefits, which may be termed *value-added* outcomes (see Exhibit 4.2).

Policies chart a course of action for the organization, set the goals and premises of the curriculum, and foster alignment between planned purpose, organizational activity, and performance evaluation. As these three elements become aligned, eventually achieving unity, Total Quality Education emerges. By getting a handle on policies, a board establishes the mechanism for quality control and clarifies for all to see what is important in the organization without getting bogged down in the details.

- Established local control, with direction for organizational operations and quality improvement
- Clear framework for control and focusing of organizational energy and resources toward the mission of the organization
- Well-defined decision-making structure, with predetermined authority and responsibility
- Provisions for long-term planning and increased productivity over time

Exhibit 4.2. Value-Added Benefits of Written Policy Supportive of Quality Improvement

Energizing Board Governance Through Policy

School boards only have so much time at their disposal. They cannot do everything that a school organization requires to operate. Using means to provide direction with minimal effort enhances board effectiveness. By focusing on the "big picture" or the overriding values and fundamental elements of the organization, the board can influence numerous issues and actions with more efficiency. For example, rather than approving specific educational field trips that are conducted for a plethora of programs or student organizations, the board can set forth principles for economy of time and resources with clear expectations for educational benefit. The board can achieve what it wants to happen in terms of the higher purpose of the school system, without getting mired down in details. Advantage and efficiency are gained.

Some board members express a strong interest in operational activities of the organization, and sometimes they try to specialize in some aspect of organizational functioning. Governance with well-designed and implemented policy obviates the need for board involvement in day-to-day operations. The "board member as expert" expectation is unrealistic and may actually impair effective governance. By staying at the conceptual or oversight level with policy, boards can be more potent in addressing those things of enduring importance. At the same time, directing the organization by clarifying expectations and purposes provides a greater likelihood for empowering staff and employees to commit to the processes of continual improvement.

Good boards spend time creating and musing about possible futures for their schools. Dealing with details and trivia of operations deflects the board from the opportunity and chance to fuel the organization with their hopes, inspiration, dreams, or vision. In effect, clarifying the value system and breathing life into it are the greatest contributions a board member can make (Carver, 1991b).

Characteristics of Quality Board Policy Governance

Given that policy determination and establishment is perhaps the most crucial responsibility for boards seeking Total Quality Education, certain policies are essential and necessary for sound governance and organizational functioning. Deming (1982) refers to avoiding "tampering" by leadership and advises changing the system as a whole, rather than incrementally through its parts. Governance in quality terms calls for deliberate board action at the "macro" or conceptual, overarching level to define the aims and purposes and to put a framework in place for quality control and implementation. The scope and content of the required policy areas are shown in Exhibit 4.3.

To be effective in supporting and fostering Total Quality Education, policies must be reduced to writing and made accessible to all participants in the system. Values and differences must be exposed and evident, and options and alternatives must be confronted openly. Policy may be extrapolated from precedent or previous actions taken, but implicit or unstated (common law) policy must be replaced with explicit policy including the criteria that underlie the policy. Policies must be simply stated, brief and not complex, centrally available, and up-to-date. If the board lives with its policies, policies will either work or get changed. Any policy that is not genuinely needed or not sincerely meant should be eliminated. Policies must mean what they say, and their words must have integrity for governance to work.

Beliefs and Values

1. Community view of the purpose of education, how the system should be run, and how people should be treated (Clemmer, 1991)
2. Clarification of expectations of curriculum approaches and requirements for board approval
3. How quality will be achieved (i.e., alignment with purpose, activities, and performance)
4. Expectations for long-term planning and goal setting
5. Roles and responsibilities of board, superintendent, and staff

Direction

1. Instructional issues (educational structure, use of time, decision-making, etc.)
2. Requirements for defined, written curriculum in all subjects and areas
3. Review processes to maintain relevant and contemporary curriculum
4. Textbook, materials, and resource selection and approval by the board

Connectivity and Equity

1. Educational services for exceptional students
2. Equal access to the curriculum
3. Curriculum development with vertical articulation and horizontal coordination
4. Continuity of the curriculum from one level to another
5. Training for staff in delivery of the curriculum
6. Requirements for monitoring the curriculum

Exhibit 4.3. Board Policy Scope and Content Essential for Quality Improvement

7. Nature and extent of support services
   a. Personnel, professional and support
   b. Buildings and grounds
   c. Food services
   d. Risk management
   e. Transportation
   f. Health and safety
8. Community relationships and participation
9. Student rights and responsibilities

Assessment and Performance Evaluation

1. Requirements for program and process assessment
2. Expectations for use of data from assessment in determining program, curriculum, and operational effectiveness and efficiency
3. Board monitoring of organizational performance
4. Formative, ongoing, process monitoring and measurement of tools and expectations

Productivity and Use of Resources

1. Budgeting and fiscal procedures, and how feedback from performance assessment is used in allocations of resources
2. Curriculum priority determinations and resource assignments
3. Environmental requirements for Total Quality Education
4. Board communication systems
5. Process control with data-driven decisions

Exhibit 4.3. Continued

The Concept of Encompassment in Quality Policy

Sometimes, policies are written for school districts in huge, compendious volumes that attempt to define the sun, the moon, the stars, and the universe for every detail of system functioning. A huge, expansive policy is not necessarily a good policy. A good policy is a guide to discretionary action and focuses on the big questions and broad issues that confront the organization. In effect, good policies are simple, short, and encompass all subelements of organizational needs. Boards can easily become bogged down in time-consuming work if policy work is not limited to the largest issues and values of the system. The inside functioning of the organization can be shaped by staying on the outside. Policy should only go as far as it needs to go, and it should stop at the point when any reasonable interpretation of the board's intentions would be acceptable.

Hierarchy of Policy Development

A sound policy is usually developed in hierarchical fashion— that is, that the board decides the overall, encompassing value first, and leaves it up to management and staff to fill in the specifics. This approach minimizes patchwork, gaps, overlaps, contradictions, and board intrusions into administrative or operational functions. It is not unlike a "mixing-bowl" concept, where the board decides issues and values from the largest to the smallest and stops once it feels that it has established proper parameters or boundaries for system functioning. For example, the board may create a policy that establishes the system mission and purpose, perhaps including a call for "competent, employable citizens." It might then define some standards or manifestations of competent, such as "academic, job-skill, and life-planning capabilities." Once this larger value is decided, the board leaves a range of choices available to management and staff, but in accordance with quality principles stated earlier in this book, the board monitors the attainment of this expected outcome systematically.

Starting with the big questions first is a clear example of sound problem solving. Staff policy then carries out board policy, and the board does not have to trap itself in a morass of complexity. Simplicity provides a form of "compelling elegance." When the number of policies is fewer than the number of decisions required, the board is better positioned to oversee and monitor the organization in more effective ways without "tampering."

When a Policy Is Not a Policy

The idea of encompassment enables the board to resolve larger issues before smaller ones and requires fewer policies. Excessive complexity stultifies quality (Peters & Waterman, 1982). By focusing on the "whole," the board governs without getting sucked into a whirlpool of the parts. However, the administration or management and staff or work teams in Total Quality Education also are going to make policy. In fact, every decision made by employees or management is policy, albeit implicit and unpublished. Everyone in the organization makes policy, and a boundary is needed. Once that is said, it is also evident that there is no set boundary between the board and management, or perhaps even management and staff. In any case, there is a difference between policy and regulations (Clemmer, 1991). These differences are displayed in Exhibit 4.4.

Once the boundary is drawn, it becomes clear that all policies (regulations) of management and staff must be consistent with broad purposes and expectations established by the governing body. Management and staff, in determining actions and making decisions, are making policy, and they must be alert to the fact that all employee actions are subject to board review. Regulations might be modified or changed if necessary to properly align with board-defined organizational values.

Monitoring Means and Progress Toward Ends

The most effective form of governance controls what needs to be controlled, yet frees what can be free (Carver, 1991a). The board does itself a favor and fosters greater opportunity for quality improvement if it limits its involvement in the operations and

Policy	Regulation
• Deals with values, aims, or goals	• Deals with facts and functions
• Establishes general direction for organization	• Specifies guidelines and defines staff responsibilities
• Answers *what* or *why* questions	• Answers *who, how, when,* or *where* questions
• Reserves a function unto the board	• Prescribes or prohibits actions or organizational behaviors
• Delegates authority and interprets expectations and ends	• Describes means more than ends
• Has roots in law, board minutes, or negotiated agreements	• Originates from management or operational handbooks
• Establishes obligations that only the board can change	• Sets forth obligations that only the superintendent can change

Exhibit 4.4. Characteristics That Differentiate Policies From Regulations in Quality Improvement

activities of the organization. The only reasons a governing board would monitor *how* things are getting done would be to assure itself that organizational behaviors are working well and are sensible, fair and just, and within legal constraints.

Adoption of regulations is not necessary and is ill-advised. Regulations are not "adopted" by anyone (Clemmer, 1991). Regulations are created, designed, developed, and implemented by the superintendent, as chief executive officer of the board. Only the superintendent may revise a regulation. Of course, if the review finds that the regulations are inconsistent with board intentions, it is up to the superintendent to manage revisions of the regulations. Also, the board may further clarify its intentions with policy revision and modification that falls short of unilaterally usurping the superintendent's regulatory function. Keeping the roles distinctly separate contributes to organizational effectiveness.

Summary

Organizational policies that contain a framework of values and perspectives are the prime undertaking of the governing board, and they affect and permeate the entire system. Values and perspectives are powerful forces that shape organizational behaviors, activities, and accomplishments. Development of policy is best if proactive as opposed to reactive. Board values parent all management and staff actions in a Total Quality Education system. The policy framework drives specific decisions and organizational functions while providing discretion for staff and management at the same time to creatively and resourcefully work for attainment of the underlying aims and purposes. Board policy, when approached from broad conceptual levels, gets a flavor of authority that escapes the trivial and mundane proceedings of the organization. Moreover, board policy gains rigor with succinctness. Governance characterized by policy focus on overall quality control diminishes the chances for reactivity or "quick fixes," bottlenecking with burdensome low-level issues, trivializing that detracts attention to more important and global issues, ritualizing by board ownership of actions that lets staff off the hook, and confusion due to disconnected short-term focus on parts rather than the whole.

Key Terms and Concepts

Encompassment. The incorporation of broad requirements and precepts for organizational functioning in an economical and uncomplicated format in policy development and design.

Policy. Principles, plans, or courses of action established, sought, and commanded by the governing body of a school system, dealing with values, aims, and desired ends, rather than means.

Regulation. A set of defined functions and guidelines that define staff responsibilities within the organization, including descriptions of means rather than ends.

Scope and content. The breadth and comprehensiveness of policies and the specific nature and characteristics of the required ends for the organization.

References

Bonstingl, J. J. (1992). *Schools of quality: An introduction to total quality management in education.* Alexandria, VA: Association for Supervision and Curriculum Development.

Brodinsky, B. (1977). *How a school board operates.* Bloomington, IN: Phi Delta Kappa Educational Foundation.

Carver, J. (1991a). *Boards that make a difference.* San Francisco: Jossey-Bass.

Carver, J. (1991b). *Recommendations to the West Virginia Legislative Oversight Commission on Education Accountability.* Carmel, IN: Carver Governance Design.

Clemmer, E. F. (1991). *The school policy handbook: A primer for school board members.* Boston: Allyn & Bacon.

Deming, W. E. (1982). *Out of the crisis.* Cambridge: MIT Press.

Downey, C. J. (1993). Focusing policy on our business—learning: Establishing curriculum quality control through policy. *Education, 113*(2), 172-175.

Downey, C. J., & Frase, L. E. (in press). *The curriculum audit and total quality management.* Lancaster, PA: Technomic.

English, F. W. (1988). *Curriculum auditing.* Lancaster, PA: Technomic.

Melvin, C. A. (1991). Restructuring schools by applying Deming's management theories. *Journal of Staff Development, 12*(3), 16-20.

Peters, T. J., & Waterman, R. H., Jr. (1982). *In search of excellence: Lessons from America's best run companies.* New York: Harper & Row.

Scherkenbach, W. W. (1991). *Deming's road to continual improvement.* Knoxville, TN: SPC Press.

✧ 5 ✧

Choosing a Quality Future

An organization that does not change rapidly becomes obsolescent and eventually becomes obsolete (Barker, 1989). Change and improvement are essential for survival. Change and improvement are not accidental—they are the result of prudent and decisive planning. Organizational direction is a product of planning, and direction is the responsibility of the governing board.

Once the board has established a strong framework of policy to guide the organization, the board is free to begin the key task of planning for the system's future. One of the important spin-off benefits of Total Quality Education is that empowerment of management and staff to handle operations and organizational functioning releases the governing board to focus on more important tasks, such as planning for, or choosing the future of, the school system.

Long-range planning is not a frill—it is one of the most important areas of trust the board has been given (Elliot, 1992). Failing to plan should more properly be regarded as planning to fail. Boards that wait until a crisis arises before they deal with the issues involved are often pushed into decisions and responses that are detrimental to the organization. Making a decision based on expedience has the likely consequence of greater damage than no decision at all (Anderson & Wendel, 1989). Anticipating issues before they arise makes for better governance and fosters quality improvement. There is an old adage that exemplifies the reactionary goverance role. It says, "When you're up to your hips in alligators, it's difficult to remember that your objective was to drain the swamp." Also, planning ahead can make the difference between success and failure. General George Patton, the eminently successful American military leader during World War II, was quoted as once saying, "It's okay to be surprised, but it's not okay to be *taken* by surprise."

Creating Vision and Constancy of Purpose

Governing boards must be visionaries for their school systems, and they must take the lead in envisioning the community's educational future. The board, in cooperation with the superintendent and teacher leaders, creates a consensus view or vision of what they believe the purpose of education to be in their community (Schlecty, 1992). Once the purpose of education is envisioned, the board must formulate the goals, define the outcomes, and set the course for its schools within the larger context of educational excellence and equity for all of its clientele (National School Board Association, 1992). This is an important leadership role for boards. People within the system need an idea of what the system stands for, what kind of educational program the community needs and wants, and where they as an organization are headed. In effect, the board has the chance to create its future.

Establishing a shared vision is only part of the journey to quality. Planning will aid the board in not only conceptualizing the vision for the system's future but in developing the necessary goals, objectives, and measures necessary to achieve that future. It is more than simply trying to forecast the future and plan accordingly (Goodstein, Nolan, & Pfeiffer, 1992). The board must grapple with questions such as, What kind of a world will our children be living in? and What knowledge, skills, and attitudes will they require to thrive in that world? (Stephens, 1993). Another way of putting it is to ask, What do we *really* want to achieve? (Senge, 1990). Given broad involvement and diverse perspectives from all customers and noncustomers of the community, the board can fashion a vision based on what students in schools today *need* in addition to what communities *want*. Both should be part of what the system as a whole values.

---

1. Booming global economy
2. Renaissance in the arts
3. "Free market socialism"
4. Global lifestyles coupled with cultural nationalism
5. Privatization of the welfare state
6. Economic force of Pacific Rim
7. Women in leadership
8. Age of biology and human longevity
9. Religious revival
10. Triumph of individual with group synergy

Exhibit 5.1. Predicted Changes in Society and the World ("Millennial Megatrends" [Naisbitt & Aburdene, 1990])

Elements of Change That Affect School Organizations

A great many forces and influences affect school institutions. The nature of the clientele is changing, the structure of families is changing, the economic demands of the marketplace are changing, and almost every part of the system as a whole is changing. Schools have had to modify what they do in order to better meet the complex and dynamic changes in the educational environment. Failing to respond would indicate an abdication of the obligation to contribute to the ongoing viability of our society, but some do resist change. However, as often noted in sports, "You are either getting worse or you are getting better—nothing stays the same." In the world today, little is staying the same. Witness the changes predicted by the turn of the century (Naisbitt & Aburdene, 1990) in Exhibit 5.1.

These changes have prompted many to theorize what they mean for schools. Schools have not changed much. One observer of schools noted that "schools are preparing graduates for a world of 20 years ago." Perhaps, if Rip Van Winkle had just awakened from a sleep of 20 years, he would find more comfort in a public school than anywhere else because of the small amount of change there (Manatt, 1991). Categorizing challenges for change in

- Relativistic values and individualism: Progress in reasoning is hampered by ideosyncratic ad hoc collections of values.

- Long-range prospects of scarcity and downward mobility: Educational skills and economic standing of future generations will be less than that of their parents.

- Time as a precious commodity: Time is increasingly traded for income, and technology pressures hamper enjoyment of life.

- Pursuit of self-fulfillment: Absorption with self causes an inability for collaborative relationships and productive cooperation.

- Redefinition of the family: Redefinition of roles results in disinvestment in development of youth.

- Personally and socially destructive behavior: Drugs, sexual abuse, suicide, and violence threaten public safety.

Exhibit 5.2. Influences That Shape and Threaten American Culture

schools produces a broad collection of shifting societal forces that affect planning. One suggested list of categories is shown in Exhibit 5.2 (Petersen, 1992).

Given the complexity of issues and changes that face society, school boards must recognize that the "worst decision is no decision" (Reecer, 1989).

Strategic Thinking in Quality Improvement

In the context of Total Quality Education, governing boards have to adopt a new philosophy and follow guidelines of strategic thinking. Precepts of strategic thinking have been identified and defined for school leaders (Valentine, 1991). Restated in terms applicable for governance, strategic thinking recognizes the following:

- Change is a permanent condition.
- A broad vision is needed of where the system is and where it should be going.
- Environmental changes must be anticipated and obstacles must be overcome.
- Intrinsic motivation is essential for the organizational team.
- Resources of the organization must be focused on achieving its goals.

What the system needs is a clear statement of vision and mission—a clear focus for organizational aims and purposes. The connection of aims and purposes and organizational activity and performance has been spelled out in quality control literature (English, Hoyle, & Steffy, 1990). Quality control involves three organizational components: purpose (aims and expectations), function (activity and work), and feedback (assessment and monitoring). These three components are depicted in the graphic displayed in Exhibit 5.3.

The relationship of purpose, function, and feedback is an ongoing one. As the mission, work standard, goals, or aims and purposes are aligned with the organization's functions, work, and activities by monitoring feedback on performance, greater quality results in the system.

Addressing Purpose Through Planning

Planning sets the framework for organizational functioning. For planning to be effective, five specifications must be met to actively address organizational needs and purposes (Flinchbaugh, 1992). These specifications are listed in Exhibit 5.4.

Planning in many cases has been haphazard, limited in its inclusion of participants, and based on inaccurate assumptions or information. Without clear aims, wide participation, legitimate data, and realistic action implementation, planning flounders.

Exhibit 5.3. Components of Organizational Quality Improvement

---

- Formulation from the perspective of the school system's purposes and aims
- Inclusion of all components and functions of the school system
- Requirement of participation of representatives from throughout the system
- Origination from valid and accurate organizational and environmental data
- Action-oriented statements of need sufficient for organizational response and applications

---

Exhibit 5.4. Specifications for Effective School Organizational Planning

---

MISSION

To provide a quality educational experience in a cooperative atmosphere where students develop to the best of their ability the academic, social, and physical skills necessary to become responsible, productive citizens who are motivated to learn.

Indianola Community School District
Indianola, Iowa 1993

Exhibit 5.5. Typical School District Mission Statement

Components of Planning

Well-conceived planning for schools begins with clarification of purpose, usually achieved with comprehensive involvement in the development of the system mission statement. A well-conceived and widely held mission gives boards an assurance that the organizational members are working from like purposes. The involvement of the organization's stakeholders in the creation of its mission increases the likelihood that the mission accurately represents the true nature of the organization and what it wants to be (Flinchbaugh, 1992). An example of a typical school district mission statement is shown in Exhibit 5.5. Although this mission statement may not be perfect, it goes a long way toward helping the organizational members and supporters understand what the organization stands for and what it hopes to do.

Organizational Mission

This is the foundation or basis for strategic planning. Everything the organization is or does stems from the common understanding of the organization's aims and purposes. Given an unclouded, prudent statement of mission, people in and related to the organization can see where the organization is headed, what it holds to be important, and what it believes it is trying to accomplish.

Assessment of Needs

Any scientific approach demands that decisions be made on the basis of performance data, not on bias, hunches, or popularity (Kaufman, 1992). Needs assessment involves gathering data about the organization (internal functioning) and the forces and influences affecting it (external environment). The information gathered must clearly define organizational strengths, weaknesses, opportunities, and threats. Innaccurate or incomplete information jeopardizes decision making and choice of future action. The planning process gets better as the relevant sources and reliable nature of information get better.

Information Analysis

Once sound and appropriate information is obtained, some sense needs to be made of what the collected data say. Effective data analysis requires highly technical skill, but better understanding of basic issues helps decision makers fashion future courses of action. Gaps between currently observed results and expectations or desired results must be identified, so that practical ways and means to meet organizational needs can be developed. A grasp of the fit between current status and the organization's aims and purposes tests the assumptions of the system and provides the basis for quality improvement.

Goal Setting

Goals are general statements of expected outcomes over a reasonably long period of time. Goals clarify the intent of the organization to improve or to change, and they indicate the priorities for primary focus of system resources. No organization can do everything at once, so goals are reasonable in number, have realistic time lines, and describe conditions that the school organization wants to reach. Goals are broad but incorporate specific objectives that not only can be reached but that are beneficial to the achievement of the organization's aims. The very nature of goals should reflect a focus on the future and change, rather than things as they currently are. Goals include measurable, self-evident criteria for determining whether or not the goal has been achieved.

Action Implementation

It is one thing to set goals; it is quite another to carry them out. Many times in the past, planning has stopped short of this step. In fact, it is one of the chief complaints about strategic planning (Flinchbaugh, 1992) by school board members. Noble intentions and lofty desired ends have been developed, only to find their way to the oblivion of some dusty shelf. It is critical to lay out the steps to be taken to work toward goals and objectives, so that the objectives, and in turn the goals, can be met. "Business as usual" must be changed. Practical actions must be designed to attack and solve problems. Someone must be made responsible for the action, and a time frame must be established, with checkpoints in process and a final time limit. Resources must be identified and provided in support of each activity planned. In this way, plans can be converted into specific courses of action and work activities.

Ongoing Assessment

Evaluation must occur before, during, and after organizational activities. A comprehensive evaluation framework must have the capability of assessing the status of activities, analyzing in-process results, and reporting outcomes to decision makers. Waiting until the process is completed before evaluating is like driving by looking in the rearview mirror (Deming, 1982). Ongoing evaluation should be occurring during each step of the process, and in fact, it should be evaluating the process itself. Monitoring activities should assess how well things are proceeding and should facilitate midstream adjustments or corrections, if needed. Another type of evaluation should be conducted at the end of the process to see if the goals or objectives have been reached. Both kinds of evaluation are too important to be left to chance. As in any sound managerial system, responsibility and time lines for expected performance should characterize evaluation processes.

Tools for Developing Quality

There are a number of technical tools and techniques used in quality engineering and statistical process control that have some degree of utility in Total Quality Education. What these tools are and how they can be of help to schools are explained below.

Cause-and-Effect Diagrams

Also called fishbone diagrams, the cause-and-effect diagrams provide a map of the factors thought to affect a problem or desired outcome. Essentially a pictorial display of a list of causes or solutions, the diagram is a "branching" set of arrows showing factors of equipment, personnel, methods, materials, and environment that pertain to problems. The diagram aids in the easy identification of factors needed to assure success in an effort or organizational undertaking.

Flowcharts

Flowcharts depict the flow of a product or a piece of information through its various steps and phases. The flowchart describes or shows most or all of the steps involved in a process, with varying levels of detail. The chart also shows loops caused by rework or recycling. Detailed flowcharts can be helpful, but the detail involved is often excessive, causing frustration among team members.

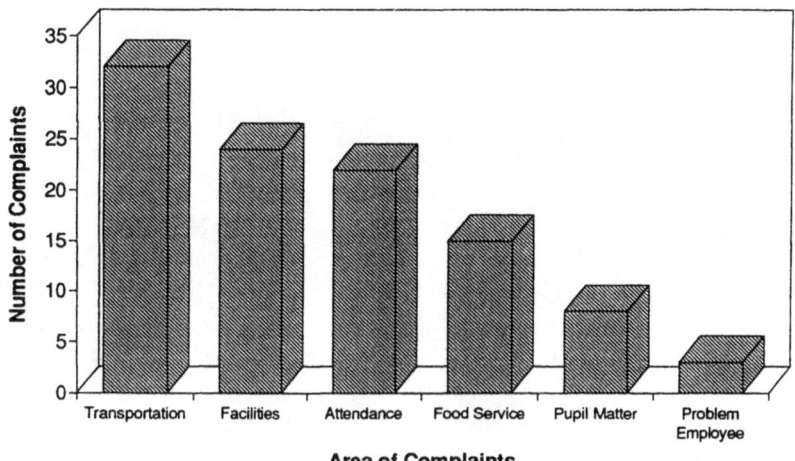

Area of Complaints

Exhibit 5.6. Sample Pareto Chart on School Complaints

Pareto Analysis Charts

Pareto charts help focus improvement efforts by ranking problems or their causes. A Pareto chart (see Exhibit 5.6) is a type of histogram with vertical bars representing the frequency or impact of problems. The bars are arranged in descending order from left to right, meaning that those on the left are more important than those on the right. The name of the technique comes from the "Pareto Principle," which states that 80% of the trouble comes from 20% of the problems.

The Pareto chart is a useful tool to determine where things are before the organization undertakes a change or improvement.

Other Types of Descriptive Charts

There are many other kinds of charts to help decision makers display data for understanding. Some of the options include run charts that monitor a process or an action for change, histogram charts that display frequency of occurrence of a variable, and

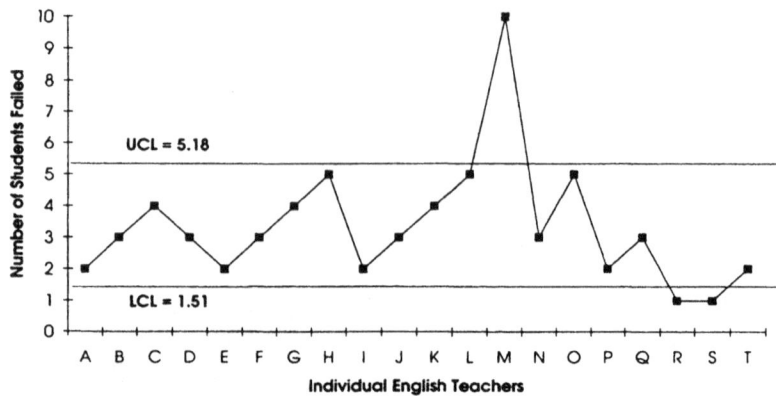

Exhibit 5.7. Sample Control Chart Tracking Student Failures in English Classes

scatter diagrams that are used to exhibit multiple occurrences of one variable in relationship to another. Force field analysis charts help identify the supporting and restraining forces of an action or a process. Many other charts are available for use in displaying descriptive information.

Control Charts

Control charts are analytical tools that are used to examine process measures to see if variability is due to common causes or random variation and how much variability is due to special causes, unique events, or individual actions. The control chart (see Exhibit 5.7) helps the decision maker determine if a situation is under statistical control or if variation is within limits ascribed to common causes. The control chart has a statistically determined upper and lower control limit, usually three standard deviations away from the norm of the measured instances.

The control chart (Type C chart) shown in Exhibit 5.7 illustrates the number of student failures in English classes by teacher for a school district with 20 English teachers. The range of failures by teacher is from 1 to 10, with a mean number of failures 3.35. The calculated upper control limit is 5.18 failures, and the lower control limit is 1.51 failures. The process is shown "out of control" because three points fall outside the control limits, indicating that failure rates may be attributable to special causes. Any number of causes might be affecting the number of student failures, but the tool is designed to identify the range of variation and to determine reasons for excessive statistical variation (Wheeler & Chambers, 1986).

Quality and the Mechanics of Planning

Planning is not a stand-alone activity. It should be part and parcel of the fabric of the entire system. Board members are the "authority" of the organization, which calls for them to conduct themselves in certain distinctive ways. An educational system is a complex network of interdependent parts, each relying on the others for support and nurturance. Each part must work effectively with all other parts to achieve organizational quality (Deming, 1982). Not unlike the human organism, each of the components work individually and in concert with all other components to make the system function as it does or should.

The board must work on system functioning to assure congruence of effort and consistency in operations. If one component of the system is operating at the expense of any other component, the system as a whole fails. All parts must work well together for success. The board should model and emulate the organization's values. Given emphasis on key educational priorities by the board, that message will permeate the rest of the organization and make it improve. However, failure to provide a shared-values system will weaken the organization.

Summary

Human organizations must see the need for preparing for the future and must work diligently and constantly to consciously do so. Planning for change is a prerequisite for survival, and if an organization does what is has always done, it should expect to get what it has always gotten. Despite this obvious condition, American schools remain remarkably resistant to change. Changing organizational ways and means to rational and systematic planning for continuous improvement will take a long time to accomplish, just as it did in American industry (Halberstam, 1986).

Despite the difficulty of the journey, governing boards control and create the future of schools as a result of the actions they take. Without rigorous, active planning, changes will occur anyway, but no guarantee will be provided that the changes will be beneficial or desirable. Planning processes avert chaos, build in continuous quality improvement, and aid the governing board in managing change for a satisfying future.

Key Terms and Concepts

Change. Any modification of organizational functioning, characteristics, or purposes based on forces and influences that affect the organization internally or externally.

Planning. The process of setting goals and implementing action based on assessment of needs, information analysis, and performance evaluation.

Quality improvement. The process of interaction and change of aims, purposes, and organizational functions resulting from continuous assessment of performance.

Quality tools. Any of a number of technical or statistical techniques used in monitoring organizational actions or characteristics useful in improvement processes.

Strategic thinking. Connections between organizational aims and purposes and activity and performance characterized by continual improvement, clarity of purpose, implementation of change, and intrinsic motivation of people involved.

References

Anderson, K. E., & Wendel, F. C. (1989). It takes more than a crystal ball to anticipate emerging policy issues. *American School Board Journal, 176*(9), 36-37.

Barker, J. A. (1989). *Discovering the future*. Lake Elmo, MN: ILI Press.

Deming, W. E. (1982). *Out of the crisis*. Cambridge: MIT Press.

Elliot, C. (1992). *Board member manual*. Frederick, MD: Aspen Publishers.

English, F. W., Hoyle, L., & Steffy, B. (1990). *Skills for successful leaders*. Arlington, VA: American Association of School Administrators.

Flinchbaugh, R. W. (1992). *The 21st century board of education: Planning, leading, transforming*. Lancaster, PA: Technomic.

Goodstein, L. D., Nolan, T. M., & Pfeiffer, J. W. (1992). *Applied strategic planning: An overview (revised)*. San Diego, CA: Pfeiffer.

Halberstam, D. (1986). *The reckoning*. New York: Avon Books.

Kaufman, R. (1992). The challenge of total quality management in education. *International Journal of Educational Reform, 1*(2), 149-165.

Manatt, R. P. (1991, October). *School transformation*. Paper presented to the Green Valley Area Education Agency, Creston, IA.

Naisbitt, J., & Aburdene, P. (1990). *Megatrends 2000: Ten new directions for the 1990's*. New York: William Morrow.

National School Board Association (NSBA). (1992). NSBA on the revitalized role of the school board. *American School Board Journal, 176*(9), 37.

Petersen, J. (1992). *Church without walls: Moving beyond traditional boundaries*. Colorado Springs, CO: Navpress.

Reecer, M. (1989). If you want to lead the way, it's nice to know where you're going. *American School Board Journal, 176*(2), 19-39.

Schlecty, P. C. (1992). Deciding the fate of local control. *American School Board Journal, 178*(11), 27-29.

Senge, P. M. (1990). The leader's new work: Building learning organizations. *Sloan Management Review, 32*(1), 7-23.

Stephens, G. M. (1993). Wrong questions lead to misdirected answers. *The School Administrator, 50*(2), 10-11.

Valentine, E. P. (1991). *Strategic management in education: A focus on strategic planning.* Boston: Allyn & Bacon.

Wheeler, D. J., & Chambers, D. S. (1986). *Understanding statistical process control.* Knoxville, TN: SPC Press.

✦ **6** ✦

Achieving Quality
Leadership and Teamwork

The 15,000 or so local school boards—traditionally venerable guardians of American educational governance and local control—are confronted with an unprecedented grim crisis of duty and relevance, and it has not escaped notice of the public. In a recent editorial about the newly selected superintendent for New York City schools, the *New York Times* pointed out that "one of the biggest obstacles to improving the schools" was the "very board that had just hired [the superintendent]" ("New Chancellor," 1993). This represents disquieting news for local school governance; however, the article pointed out that the New York school board had some serious flaws in its roles and relationships. Some of these problems included the following:

- Internal politics and divisiveness
- Meddling in managerial matters
- Does poorly in primary responsibility of setting overall policy for the system

These very words could be written about the so-called typical school board in America. Boards in America have more often than not shown "frequent conflict among members, an incapacity to exhibit cooperation with leadership, progressive expansion into management, and an intrinsic inability to focus on education issues" (Twentieth Century Fund Task Force, 1992, p. 71).

Make no mistake, boards are important, and there is hidden power in quality leadership. However, Deming's ideas of quality leadership call for different roles for leaders—in this case, board members and their chief executive officer or superintendent. The quality management team, composed of the board and the superintendent, behaves in different ways. The quality management team is exemplified by restructured relationships, and the work of the team focuses on helping people do the best job possible (Scholtes, 1988).

With quality leadership principles, board deliberations and superintendent recommendations for action are undergirded with useful and relevant performance data, not opinions or guesswork. However, to make quality leadership work properly, the board and the superintendent must recognize that at least 85% of any organization's failures are the fault of management (Juran, 1988). Therein lies the challenge for boards and superintendents—work must be based on improving quality of the system, not trying to pin blame on anyone. Driving out fear is a part of the new leadership collaboration, and it shifts the emphasis from misguided focus to regaining prominence in performance.

Principles of Quality Leadership

Quality improvement withers and dies in an adversarial climate. The challenges to leadership have been exacerbated by the deterioration of the relationships between boards and superintendents to the point that 95% of the big-city superintendencies in America were vacant during all or part of the year (Wagner, 1992). On the other hand, given proper involvement and a healthy, mutually respectful and trusting relationship, better design, delivery, and improvement of all elements of the educational process can be achieved. The specific principles for quality leadership are delineated in Exhibit 6.1.

1. Client focus
2. Commitment to quality
3. Analysis of enterprise
4. Empowerment of staff
5. Shared and common vision
6. Ongoing improvement process
7. Cooperation and teamwork
8. Staff development

Exhibit 6.1. Principles of Quality Leadership

Client Focus

The school system's chief goal should be delivery of learning and curriculum (product) to the client (customer)—the student. It goes without saying that the schools are only going to be as good as students, parents, and the community think they are. If students and the community think that the schools are meeting or exceeding student needs and the programs and services are providing lasting value to the client, then the organization is probably meeting its chief goal. Of course, customers are not only external to the schools or those who use the products and services. Customers also mean internal clients, including employees, whose work and contributions depend on others in the system.

Commitment to Quality

Everyone in the schools should be imbued with a high commitment and enthusiasm for quality. All services, programs, and operations of the system should be characterized by a zeal for meeting the customer's needs, exceeding the customer's needs, and delighting the customer. Organizational productivity, as well as effectiveness and efficiency, should be sought in all aspects and functioning of the system by all who are a part of its processes and operations.

Analysis of Enterprise

Excellence in schools is no accident. All operations of the system are based on structure and specific activities. The enterprise, work, and activities of the system must be studied, dissected, measured, scrutinized, and evaluated for improvement. Leadership should have the responsibility to monitor all factors that affect or influence functions and operations both inside and outside of the school system. Process data, not to be confused with summative or final results, help improve the means of the organization. The focus should be on deeper understanding of the organization, rather than on evaluating the performance of individuals (remember, "drive out fear").

Empowerment of Staff

In Total Quality Education, sufficient freedom of action and discretion is provided to employees to permit creative and powerful improvement of work. Employees should not only be charged with the authority to make decisions but with the responsibility for the results of the decisions. The lowest level possible in the organization should be targeted for delegation of operational decision making and responsibility. Given appropriate empowerment, potential problems can be anticipated and addressed early and quickly by those who confront and deal with them first.

Shared and Common Vision

Focused attention on a commonly held vision of the organization is like a "glue" that bonds people together. Shared vision enables the organization's people to move in accord with one another toward an organization that they have been able to picture in their minds (Ciampa, 1992). Board members build vision among others in the organization by looking beyond the day-today stream of events to the values that underlie those events. Focusing on values, communicating high loyalty to the mission of the system, and keeping purposes and expectations for clients above all else sends a message and an example to every nook and cranny of the organization. In short, a board can successfully lead by nurturing its corporate support and commitment to big dreams and lucid values and by maintaining fidelity to this role (Carver, 1990). More about fidelity to the board role is discussed in a later section on relationships. The board is in a better position than any other group to foster and exemplify a view of the sort of school system that could be.

Ongoing Improvement Process

There is risk in believing that "if it ain't broke, don't fix it." The best time, and perhaps the least difficult time, is to work on improving the system when things appear to be functioning well. If improvement is undertaken when problems are rampant, or when a crisis overshadows the organization, the board has to operate from a less effective reactive stance. Improvement should be continuous. Deming would say there is no other way —"you get good solid data and learn how to interpret what the data tell you. It's common sense. There is no other way" (Deming, 1992, quotation from his presentation *Quality, Productivity, and Competitive Position* to the Quality Enhancement Seminar).

As the board focuses on better and better performance throughout the organization, it is being true to tomorrow more than to today or even yesterday. Consequently, the pursuit of quality is a perpetual task, and the definition of quality never stands still. Constant change can be discomforting, probably because of the fear that comes from being in between what has worked well in the past and the new way of doing things that lies ahead and is yet unknown. It is not unlike being "in between trapezes" (Ferguson, 1980). The challenge for the board is to recognize that comfort with the status quo will eventually make the organization obsolescent. Quality leadership also realizes that at least 85% of an organization's failures are the fault of management and board-directed systems (Deming, 1982). Given that foundation, the board's focus should be on constant and rigorous improvement processes and on looking for faults or difficulties that need correction or improvement.

Cooperation and Teamwork

Anyone who has visited Disney World or Disneyland recognizes that workers can be happy at what they do, everyone can be going in the same direction, problems can be anticipated, and an organization can be one big happy family (Ciampa, 1991). Such an organization, with trust and teamwork, cannot be built overnight, but experience in the private sector has shown that teamwork works. As school systems tackle the challenges of the quality movement, they discover the benefits of having people at all levels working together in teams. Of course, what is good for the goose is good for the gander. The board should also focus on team-building activities so it can weld together an effective unit focused on common purposes, sharing ownership of ideas, and mutual trust in resolving conflicts amicably. What makes a competent board is the strength of interpersonal development *as a group* (Chait, Holland, & Taylor, 1992). The more the board works together, establishes group goals, and attends to its collective strength, the more effectiveness it garners in its quest for Total Quality Education.

Staff Development

Investing in greater skills and understandings about the right things often provides a dramatic and substantial return in a school organization. Total Quality Education demands a vigorous program of education and self-improvement for all participants, including board members. Everyone in the organization must know and understand his or her job and role in the organization and how the roles change as quality improves (Scholtes, 1988). This is a big undertaking. Interrelationships of tasks, coordination across grade levels, articulation within learning content areas, skills for improving work, and understanding issues that confront the organization are factors to be addressed in staff development and training efforts. Improving quality in education requires new skills. Training and development of new skills should incorporate iden- tifying purpose, clarifying work roles, assessing performance, studying and drawing implications from data, planning and man- agement techniques, instructional efficacy, and group leadership skills, to name a few.

Seven Deadly Diseases That Stand in the Way of Quality

Deming (1982) cites seven "diseases" that block progress in quality transformation. In Total Quality Education, some of the diseases are more relevant than are others. The diseases are listed in Exhibit 6.2.

The implications of the seven deadly diseases are perhaps obvious to governing boards. However, key thoughts for board members might entail the points that are stated in Exhibit 6.3. Although the seven deadly diseases originally referred to private sector business organizations, the premises and nature of them apply to Total Quality Education. Giving attention to the message of the diseases can go a long way toward achieving quality im- provement in a school system.

Board-Superintendent Relationships

There are few issues in school governance more thorny than defining the line between board responsibilities and superinten- dent responsibilities. The line is often fuzzy, and the negative impact of role confusion or "invading the other's turf" is detrimental to any school organization. Findings from a survey revealed that three out of five board members and three out of four superinten- dents believe they do not know where to draw the line between policy and administration (Wagner, 1992). In Total Quality Educa- tion, the roles are distinctively and appropriately defined to pro- vide congruence and consistency in governance, management, and organizational operations. Although the superintendent is responsible for the daily management and operation of the school

1. Lack of constancy of purpose: Proper commitment to planning and activity monitoring will keep the organization alive and well.

2. Emphasis on short-term profits (thinking): Looking for quick fixes or short-term solutions may harm the organization in the long run.

3. Personal review, or merit pay, systems: Intrinsic motivational techniques are far superior to extrinsic motivation based on fear, rewards, quotas, or objectives.

4. Instability and excessive mobility of top management: The short average time of tenure of board members and superintendents impairs continuity and long-range development of quality.

5. Use of visible figures only for management: Limiting data sources on performance to standardized test scores, financial statements, or inadequate measures leaves much of the organization in the dark or unknown.

6. Excessive medical costs: Increases in the costs of benefits jeopardize investment in improvement of organizational functioning.

7. Excessive costs of liability: Risk exposures for public institutions have increasingly become more expensive and threaten investment in improvement.

Exhibit 6.2. The Seven Deadly Diseases

system, his or her respective role is frequently poorly defined by the board, causing confusion and disruption of sound organizational functioning.

Defining Who Does What

It is easy to say that the role of the board is to set policy, whereas the superintendent's role is to manage (Elliot, 1992).

- Maintain commitment to purpose and mission. In effect, keep "your eye on the ball."
- Look at the long view. Set up and maintain long-range planning for the system.
- Provide intrinsic evaluation support. Remove barriers from feeling good about "a job well-done."
- Keep leadership stable. Find and keep top quality leadership at the board level and in the superintendency.
- Design and use comprehensive assessment. There is much to know about any organization, and all of it helps improvement efforts.
- Control operational costs. Seek and develop effective measures to minimize costs that affect the organization as much as possible.

Exhibit 6.3. Applications of the Seven Diseases for Boards

However, drawing the line in school organizations is seldom easy. Coming to agreement on who does what is essential. The line must be drawn carefully and clearly. Clarity of roles builds confidence, generates ownership of responsibility, and provides a basis for systematic improvement over time.

Board Responsibilities and Roles

The board's primary responsibility is to clearly determine the nature of the organization's purpose—what the school should accomplish with and for its clientele. As a collective governing body, the board is responsible for planning, overseeing, and evaluating organizational operations and goals. The board must function as a team, recognizing that individual board members have neither the right nor the power to exercise any direct authority with the superintendent or any staff member. Collective team decisions are the only decisions that can legitimately be made by the board. Specific solutions to problems are best left to the superintendent

- Explicit interpretation and clarification of fundamental organizational values—what the system stands for and expects to accomplish
- Focused definitions of expectations, ends, and standards or outcomes for the organization
- Translation of organizational values into a policy that prescribes what the organization should or should not do
- Long-term viewpoints for future development and direction, including strategic planning
- Establishment of priorities and separation of big issues and important matters from trivialities of organizational operations
- Performance data accumulation and analysis to monitor and to draw implications about effectiveness, efficiency, productivity, and quality
- Development of healthy relationships and understanding of organizational aims among key constituencies
- Nurturance of the board as a team, establishing team goals, attending to the board's collective strength, and contributing to the board's growth and self-improvement
- Employment of a chief executive officer to carry out the legal and policy requirements and purposes of the organization under the board's supervision

Exhibit 6.4. Specific Roles and Responsibilities of Governing Boards

and the superintendent's staff. Basically, the board's duties and responsibilities should center on the points that are itemized in Exhibit 6.4.

Once the board has clearly determined and defined the purposes and desired ends for the school organization, it then must communicate its expectations to the superintendent. The board must spell out what it wants in terms of desired outcomes and aims to its chief executive officer and then hold the superintendent responsible and accountable for managing the system toward those ends.

Superintendent Roles and Responsibilities

Within the principles of prudence and ethics and the established policy framework from the board, the superintendent serves as the chief executive officer of the board and functions as its representative in managing the organization. The superintendent is held accountable by the board for developing ways and means to achieve the board's stated expectations. The superintendent needs discretionary authority and power to carry out the executive responsibilities without interference from the board. The superintendent cannot serve several masters but should expect to serve the board in collective deliberations and activities. The key responsibilities of the superintendent are spelled out in Exhibit 6.5.

A superintendent should be the "only" employee of the board. The superintendent is the head of all other employees in the organization. This concept is critical for boards not only to maintain continuity in the chain of command but also to properly assign responsibility in terms of organizational functions. If something goes wrong, board members should have no connection with employees in the organization except through the superintendent or at the superintendent's discretion. The characteristic differences between boards' and superintendents' responsibilities are depicted in Exhibit 6.6.

Because of its encompassing nature, the role of the superintendent can be described in a very brief job description: The superintendent is accountable to the board for implementation and accomplishment of aims and purposes defined and set forth as "ends" in board policies within the limitations of executive authority assigned by the board in policy.

Sorting Out Policy From Management

Total Quality Education depends on clear understandings of roles and responsibilities. However, once those definitions and

- Accept the accountability of the position and job responsibilities pursuant to overall performance of the organization
- Possess expertise in operational management and leadership of the organization
- Direct and manage all operations, programs, and services of the organization, including gathering data about system performance and behavior
- Share important knowledge with members of the board to keep them informed about all aspects of system functioning
- Assist the board in developing and establishing explicit and succinct policies that address the topmost levels of organizational values
- Implement and accomplish provisions of board policy through the exercise of discretionary decision making and delegation of authority
- Serve within appropriate ethical and prudent managerial processes as the board's representative within established executive limitations

Exhibit 6.5. Specific Roles and Responsibilities of the Superintendent

understandings are achieved between the superintendent and the board, it is important to keep the roles separate and distinct. Policy role decisions are those that are required by law or regulatory agencies; those that determine programs, services, operations, or processes that will govern the organization; or those that are brought to the board by the superintendent for a decision.

Regulations, or management decisions are those that relate to the workings or the activities of a specific program, service, or organizational unit (such as a school); those that relate to an individual employee; and those that deal with administrative duties or responsibilities in specific units, departments, or operations of the system.

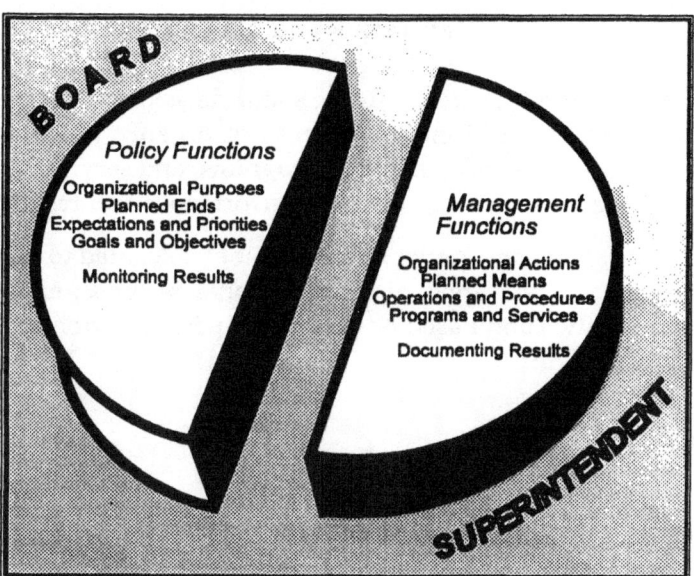

Exhibit 6.6. Roles of the Governing Board and the Superintendent Showing Separate Policy and Management Functions

Summary

School boards hold the keys to successful and effective governance. Fulfilling the governance role demands clarification of leadership roles and responsibilities for both the board and its chief executive officer, the superintendent. For optimal working relationships, the governing board should focus on policy functions, including setting organizational purposes, planning expectations and goals for the system, and monitoring results of organizational performance. Superintendent functions are twofold: (a) carry out board policies and produce results and outcomes congruent with policy requirements, and (b) manage and direct the organization in accordance with established board policies. The board and the superintendent should clarify and negotiate the line between policy and regulation, policy and management, and ends and means to gain efficiency and consistency between board and superintendent actions demonstrated in system functioning.

Key Terms and Concepts

Management functions. Actions and decisions delegated to the chief executive officer in the areas of organizational activities, means, procedures, operations, programs, and services, including gathering and documentation of performance and results.

Policy functions. Actions and decisions relegated to the governing board in the areas of organizational purpose, expectations, and priorities and based on planning and evaluation of performance and results.

References

Carver, J. (1990). *Boards that make a difference: A new design in leadership in nonprofit and public organizations.* San Francisco: Jossey-Bass.

Chait, R., Holland, T., & Taylor, B. (1992). *The effective board of trustees.* Phoenix, AZ: Oryx.

Ciampa, D. (1991). *Total quality.* New York: Addison-Wesley.

Ciampa, D. (1992). *Total quality: A user's guide for implementation.* New York: Addison-Wesley.

Deming, W. E. (1982). *Out of the crisis.* Cambridge: MIT Press.

Deming, W. E. (1992, October). *Quality, productivity, and competitive position.* Paper presented to the Quality Enhancement Seminar, St. Louis, MO.

Elliot, C. (1992). *Board member manual.* Frederick, MD: Aspen Publishers.

Ferguson, M. (1980). Untitled presentation. In J. Carver, *Boards that make a difference: A new design in leadership in nonprofit and public organizations* (p. 209). San Francisco: Jossey-Bass.

Juran, J. M. (1988). *Juran on planning for quality.* New York: Free Press.

New chancellor, old politics (Editorial). (1993, August 31). *The New York Times,* p. A10.

Scholtes, P. M. (1988). *The team handbook: How to use teams to improve quality.* Madison, WI: Joiner Associates.

Twentieth Century Fund Task Force. (1992). *Facing the challenge: The report of the Twentieth Century Fund Task Force on school governance.* New York: Twentieth Century Fund.

Wagner, R. F., Jr. (1992). The case for local education policy boards. *Phi Delta Kappan, 74*(3), 228-229.

✧ 7 ✧

Board Oversight Responsibilities

It is not enough to set the overall purpose and plans for an organization, to establish values and expectations in policy, and to empower the employees to meet customer needs. More is needed. Boards must exercise organizational oversight, or control, to assure continuous quality improvement. Control in the context of oversight means working to make all organizational efforts and activity directed toward established, specific ends (English, 1988). All staff, programs, services, activities, and resources must be focused toward the predetermined purposes of the organization. If the board does not exercise oversight, the organization's work becomes fragmented and disjointed (perhaps even contradictory), and the organization is not in "control of itself."

If local control of schools is to be preserved in terms of an accessible and workable form of government, the oversight role is a critical responsibility for governing boards. The report of the Task Force on Governance was most emphatic on this point, saying, "We cannot stress too often that the role of (boards) would be to establish policy and provide policy oversight, not to implement policy in detail" (Twentieth Century Fund Task Force, 1992, p. 9). In quality improvement terms, the energy, efforts, and means of the organization must operate in concert as a system. Systems are like the human body, functioning as a total organism despite its composition of many separate and distinct parts (Poston, 1993). If the parts are optimized, or working together, the body or system functions effectively. If the parts are working independently and uncooperatively, disarray and confusion can result, causing the body or system to become dysfunctional.

Systems Thinking and Process

Everything the board or the people of the school organization do can be described in terms of a process. The importance of this statement is self-evident. If a board does not buy into the notion that everything that occurs in the school organization is a part of a system or process, then the board is unable to improve that process. The process, or system, is virtually everything that happens or fails to happen in the school organization. In its simplest form, a process is the transformation of inputs into outputs (Scherkenbach, 1991). The system comprises five major components, which are both inputs and outputs of the process:

- People
- Method
- Material
- Equipment
- Environment

Scherkenbach (1991) suggests that these components reflect the voice of the customer as inputs and the voice of the process as outputs. If the outputs and the inputs are one and the same, unity is achieved between the process and the customer needs, and quality meets expectations.

Whether the board hires a superintendent to manage the day-to-day operation of the system, sets budget and spending priorities, establishes policies for hiring or purchasing, or approves construction projects, it does it through a process. Of course, a myriad of factors and components make up educational systems, which exhibit complex interdependent relationships. However, looking at the elements in an educational system provides a framework for oversight responsibility in governance. The major responsibilities in oversight include the tasks that are listed in Exhibit 7.1.

- Board leadership and behavior
- Policy and organizational purpose (see chapter 3)
- Organizational goals and planning (see chapter 5)
- Superintendent's leadership and performance
- Curriculum content and design
- Curriculum implementation and delivery
- Human resources and relationships
- Material resources and productivity
- Assessment and organizational performance

Exhibit 7.1. Areas of System Process for Board Oversight

A board committed to Total Quality Education would not be involved in the day-to-day operation of the system but would leave that to the chief executive officer (superintendent). The board would not be involved in the hiring of personnel, except in setting personnel policies for sound and appropriate practices. The board would not be involved in contracting and purchasing but would establish policy and hire independent auditors to review policy execution. The board would not manage or attempt to intervene in school system functioning, except at the governance level. For example, school law may require the board to approve construction bids or contracts, but it would be pointless for the board to attempt to manage the procedures in construction of a school building. The important goal is to free the board for the primary task of creating, monitoring, and overseeing system policy in terms of organizational performance.

Board Leadership and Behavior

The aim of the board's leadership should be to improve the performance of people and equipment, to improve quality, to increase productivity, and to instill pride and joy of achievement throughout the system and among its customers (Deming, 1982).

- Focus on the client: connecting the school system with the community at large and with the needs of its clientele in particular and actualizing everyone with clarity and constancy of purpose
- Establishment of governing policies: affirming the values and expectations of the system, especially desired ends, constraints, processes, and linkages
- Monitoring system performance: evaluating executive leadership against performance expectations and assuring improvement of the system

Exhibit 7.2. Essential Board Responsibilities and Duties

Quality starts and ends at the top—the board makes or breaks the system's chances for quality. The board must lead with a constancy of purpose manifested in a value-centered mission statement. The board must focus on improving productivity across the system, reaping all possible benefit from investment and costs. The development of people should reflect high commitment to ongoing improvement and support.

Board self-study and reflection on its own performance as a team is time well spent, and investing in board training and skill improvement is money well spent. There is nothing more important to the quality of the school organization than the quality of its governance. Allocations should be set aside for board training, state and national conferences, and board training materials and retreats. Retreats are excellent vehicles for dreaming and envisioning new initiatives and process improvements. The board oversees a substantial amount of community assets and owes it to those whom it serves to learn how to do the job right (Elliot, 1993).

The Board's Minimal Job Description

The minimum tasks of governance have been defined and delineated and are composed of three chief duties (or job products) of the board (Carver, 1990). Restated in terms of Total Quality Education, they are listed in Exhibit 7.2.

Evaluation is more critical for the board, because of its high visibility to internal and external publics of the organization. If the board makes sincere efforts to function effectively as a team and uses evaluation to improve its performance, the system is likely to emulate and reflect the board's behavior. The pursuit of quality is a worthy thing to do, and the board can solve practical problems through a process of inquiry into the relationship between theory and practice (Holt, 1993). Collaborative problem solving produces two distinct advantages: Better decisions are generated and ownership and commitment are logical consequences of involvement in the process.

What Boards Really Do

Board members report frustration in the work they end up doing that keeps them from important job tasks. One study revealed that local boards, on average, make only 3% of their decisions on basic policy issues. The other 97% of the time they are coping with routine procedural business, budget questions, personnel matters, and student requests (Wagner, 1992). In another study, boards were found to spend less than 4% of their time on educational improvement policy issues (Nowakowski & First, 1989). Wasting time on trivial matters has in many cases rendered boards impotent and ineffective.

BOARD FUNCTIONING CAN DISRUPT GOVERNANCE

Board member activities on occasion can interfere with sound governance. Comments from some school personnel illustrate this point, as they describe their board members (Frase, 1993, p. 13):

"One board member disciplined a staff member."

"The board is into day-to-day operations."

"We (principals) get lots of calls from board members for information."

"If a board member comes out (to my school) and I tell them [sic] about problems, they [sic]get them taken care of."

"When I need something, chairs, lights, tables, desks, etc., our board member will get it for us [sic]."

At times, it is apparent that board members assume administrative responsibility in some school systems, particularly in personnel and facilities management functions.

MEETING AGENDAS MAY INCLUDE UNNECESSARY ITEMS

The lists of items that appear on board agendas are often long and filled with things that unnecessarily consume inordinate amounts of board time. For example, in one study, the board agenda of a large-city school system contained 347 items in 20 separate agendas, of which only 21 (6.7%) dealt directly with curriculum and policy, whereas 93.6% dealt with basic administrative matters such as bids, facility agreements, gifts to schools, human resource reports, field trips, certification of expenditures, bid recessions, resolutions, minutes, and schedules (Frase, 1993).

BOARD WORK CAN BE NONESSENTIAL TO GOVERNANCE

The things a board should not do have been spelled out clearly in recent analytical reports (Frase, 1993). These reports indicate that boards should not engage in the activities that are listed in Exhibit 7.3.

In the study of board functioning discussed earlier, of the 347 items reviewed in 20 board meetings, 201 were recommended to be avoided by boards in national reports (Frase, 1993). This imbalance of activities is illustrated in Exhibit 7.4.

Unnecessary and unproductive agenda items prevent the board from dealing with important matters of board governance, including policy development, curriculum oversight, and long-range planning. If board governance is ever to be effective in delivering

- Preside over student or employee grievances
- Approve all competitive contracts and purchase orders
- Approve specific payment of expenditure items in approved budgets
- Approve construction change orders unless they have a major impact on board policy
- Hire, terminate, or promote specific personnel, except for the superintendent
- Approve detailed operational items such as field trips, staff development activities, and bus routes

Exhibit 7.3. Activities Boards Should *Not* Carry Out

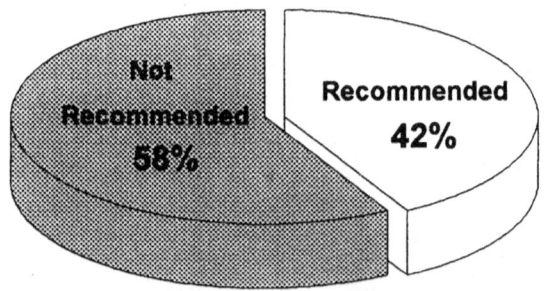

Exhibit 7.4. Percentage of Board Meeting Agenda Items Recommended or Not Recommended by National Reports

quality to a system, unproductive uses of board time and inappropriate activities of board members must be eliminated.

Building Quality Improvement Through Oversight

Shifting the board from micromanagement trivia to quality improvement focus requires not only an obsession with the process of quality improvement but continual reappraisal of the board's

1. Does the board set quality targets and provide the means for attaining them? (Moving toward organizational purpose?)
2. Does the board monitor the implementation of appropriate strategies? (Reviewing organizational performance?)
3. Does the board conduct regular appraisals of performance in association with its overall results? (Checking the value of its organizational governance?)

Exhibit 7.5. Questions for Board Evaluation

work. One way to conduct this reappraisal is to answer the three questions (Organization for Economic Cooperation and Development, 1987) listed in Exhibit 7.5.

The challenge here is to focus on performance in evaluation, not to become involved in the administrative minutiae of the system. The upshot is that excellence in governance involves refocusing the efforts of the board on the system as a whole, not immersion in the details and specifics of operations.

The board must continually conduct self-appraisal and work on its own professional and governance improvement. External reviews of performance also provide objective, criterion-based assessments of board functioning and performance. To improve the governance performance of the board, it is imperative to work at setting goals (planning), implementing strategies (doing), checking results and progress (studying), and making modifications for improvement (acting). Improvements in governance are a natural extension of the quality process when it is applied to the board.

Oversight of Superintendent's Leadership and Performance

The superintendent is the most important employee in the system for two reasons: First, he or she is the executive and professional agent of the governing board to the system, and second, he or she is the only "employee" of the board. The board's governance consists of many indispensable functions as indicated earlier in this text, and one of the more important functions is the employment of the superintendent, who should be held accountable for organizational performance. Of course, holding the superintendent responsible means that the board first has to give the superintendent not only the authority but also the wide discretionary power to do the job.

The Superintendent's Job in Relationship to the Board

Superintendents often have long and detailed job descriptions. In essence, the job descriptions make the superintendent responsible for the "sun, moon, and stars" in the school universe. However, greater specificity is helpful in clarifying the role and responsibilities of the superintendent *and* the nature of the board-superintendent relationship. The division of labor between the board and the superintendent is the determinant of optimum organizational effectiveness.

Basically, the board's chief responsibility is confined to establishing overall policies for the system, leaving the development of procedures and processes to carry out the policies up to the superintendent. All board authority delegated to staff is delegated first to the superintendent, so the superintendent can effectively manage the system. Just as the superintendent draws authority and gives accountability to the board, staff members draw their authority and provide accountability to the superintendent. This is the fundamental characteristic of a properly configured chain of command. The superintendent can provide the board with a foundation of excellence, given sound design of the role and functions.

The superintendent is accountable for all of the parts of the system coming together in a connected, holistic manner. As a result of this "funneling" of activity to one position, the job description would contain four major elements (Carver, 1991) as interpreted in Exhibit 7.6.

These job expectations are manifestations of the unity-of-command principle. The areas clearly define board and superintendent job

1. Accountability and responsibility: The superintendent should be authorized to carry out the established policies of the governing board. Any actions or activities, congruent with the spirit and intent of board policy, should be within the discretionary power of the superintendent. The board, of course, may expect to obtain reports and information about decisions and specific actions from the superintendent on a regular basis to be informed as to how its intentions are being achieved. The effectiveness of accountability in this relationship is a product of the board's trust and empowerment of the superintendent.

2. Authority and direction: The board, in corporate session and by majority vote, exercises authority over the superintendent. If individual board members expect or are permitted to give direction or make requests of the superintendent, confusion and contradiction can undermine the accountability process. Board policy ensures governance congruity and executive vigor by strictly limiting direction or exercise of authority by the board to legally convened sessions where the team functions as a team or corporate unit.

3. Limitations and constraints: Unlawful or unethical actions generally are proscribed in the policy and the definitions of the superintendent's job. A common standard in such cases is to clearly prohibit any act that is incompatible with state and federal laws, any actions that might fail to sufficiently withstand the "prudent person" test, executive actions contrary to board policy, regulatory agencies with valid jurisdiction, or fund source requirements. All constraints and limitations on executive authority require specific delineation in the superintendent's job description.

4. Communication and review: On occasion, actions taken by the superintendent may not be addressed in board policy. Also, actions taken may sometimes be contrary to written policy, when justifiable in the judgment of the superintendent. In all cases of executive action, it is incumbent on the superintendent to keep the board informed. The board, in its discretion, may approve or disapprove the action, but such action neither rescinds executive decisions nor exempts the superintendent from ensuing board judgment or evaluation of the superintendent's efficacy and performance.

Exhibit 7.6. Suggested Expectations for Delegation to the Superintendent

roles and relationships, even to the point of permitting executive action to digress from policy. It should come as no surprise that boards occasionally find that executive decisions that are based on sound judgment and that produce acceptable results actually contradict board policy. In such instances, openness and trust can still be sustained between the board and its executive officer. Clarity of the formal roles reduces to the superintendent's accountability for accomplishing the defined expectations of the board expressed in policy within the constraints and limitations of executive authority also expressed in policy. Although the board and the superintendent have separate roles, formal definition of the distinct jobs of each contributes to the strength of the leadership team.

Overseeing the Superintendent's Job in Quality Improvement

The superintendent is accountable for the entire school system working up to organizational aims and purposes. Quality improvement has been demonstrated in organizations characterized by certain leadership behaviors and actions. In short, what the leader does or does not do makes a critical difference in whether or not an organization improves over time. In quality improvement, some efforts have succeeded, whereas others have failed, and it is possible to identify key variables that have made the difference (Ciampa, 1991). For the superintendent, such findings are instructive as to what the job of the chief executive officer is in order to gain improvement in organizational quality.

Vision and Focus

Specific behaviors from the superintendent affect quality improvement. Sincere and credible commitment to customer satisfaction is demonstrated in behavior throughout the organization starting from the top. The system needs to see that quality improvement is a serious undertaking of the organization, that it can and will work, and that it is not "just another program." Unless the superintendent believes in quality improvement and projects that belief, it is unlikely to work. If, on the other hand, the superintendent has a clear mental picture of what the system can be and uses quality improvement processes to get it there, success can be realized. Everyone in the organization needs to share in the leader's vision of what the system can and should be.

Assessment and Analysis

Quality improvement depends on the gathering of data and analysis of those data for decisions for organizational action. Decisions in quality improvement are "data driven." That is, needs are determined based on best available information, processes (not discrete parts) are assessed in terms of efficacy and workability through visible effects and performance outcomes, and data are treated with openness, trust, and fearlessness in a process of study, understanding, and action. Data are data, but in public institutions they are often viewed as threats. If data are threats, then axioms such as, "Kill the messenger" or "Cover up the truth," may characterize the organization. Data must be seen as opportunities and challenges. If information causes fear, improvement is stultified.

Improvement builds on the analysis of findings about program effectiveness, materials potency, learner outcomes, teaching strategy success rates, cost and benefits, and many other system quality indicators subjected to study and scrutiny. Many statistical and analytical tools are available and useful for this purpose.

Collaborative Decision Making

Once analysis is put into place, decisions can be made for organizational improvement. Decisions are best made for quality improvement in specific ways. Teams, representing the whole process or all parts of the process, are involved in decision making using information generated from assessment and analysis. This calls for a collaborative facilitation role on the part of the superintendent. Motivation and quality of decisions are both enhanced when the superintendent can effectively build decision-making structures with broad-based involvement of the people responsible.

Application and Modeling

The quality improvement superintendent provides an environment where creative ideas and decisions can be tried in real-life situations. Pilot testing of programs and services on a limited scale yields a strong example of commitment to improvement. By implementing change on an incremental, trial basis, gaps in knowledge can be closed and the team involved can learn new behaviors and ways of doing things. Experimentation provides an excellent opportunity for learning new and better ways of operating, and support of applications and changes emphasizes a model of action dedicated to improvement.

Development and Reinforcement

A sound organization is a learning organization (Senge, 1990). While learning new ways of doing things, both the superintendent and the work team develop greater and greater expertise in an atmosphere of mutual regard. Ongoing targeted staff development enhances the ongoing efforts of people in the quest for quality. Based on the particular and specific needs of the people involved and the organization, developmental activities reinforce the quality movement. There is no substitute for training, especially that which is relevant and pinpointed at the people's needs in the quality improvement process.

Institutionalization

The last factor in quality improvement for the superintendent to work on is making changes permanent and cementing commitment to the ongoing process. The superintendent works at altering the basic operational processes of the system to incorporate collegial support and management and on visible reinforcement of quality principles. The superintendent must integrate quality improvement themes (focus on customer, constancy of purpose, etc.) into system operations and culture. A hallmark of Total Quality Education is a superintendent who is serious about quality improvement and that direction is toward improvement of instructional efficacy, service, and satisfaction of the clientele and expanded involvement of everyone into the movement.

There is no best way to implement Total Quality Education from the superintendent's office. Nevertheless, the leadership of the chief executive officer is essential in making it a reality in any school system. The principles above have been shown to be effective in producing continual quality improvement. Incorporation of them into system operations and administrative behaviors never ends in building quality into schools.

Overseeing Quality Improvement

Quality improvement in any school system is based on a clear vision of what the system should be like in terms of its customer focus, purpose, operational character, and current standing. A number of key areas require oversight by the board, but the operational responsibilities for these areas rest with the superintendent and staff. However, a grasp of what these components of quality improvement are is instructive to the board and helpful in policy formulation. The areas for oversight by the board include curriculum content and design, curriculum implementation and delivery, assessment of organizational performance, human resources and relationships, and material resources and productivity.

Curriculum Content and Design

The curriculum is the primary product of the school system. Its quality and nature significantly affect the satisfaction of the customer's needs. Curriculum in many schools is undesignated, random, and chaotic (English, 1988). Teachers are sometimes confused by what the curriculum really is, so they are often left to their own devices to determine not only how things are taught but what is taught. If the school board has no interest in establishing specific destinations for students to arrive at on completion of their journey through the schools, no curriculum design, articulation, or coordination is necessary. However, if you do not know where you are going, how will you know when you get there?

1. Scope or coverage of grade levels and content areas with written curriculum guides: What percentage of the curriculum has a curriculum guide available?

2. Quality of the curriculum guides: How good are the curriculum guides?

   a. Clear and valid objectives?

   b. Curriculum congruent with testing?

   c. Objectives defined by grade, level, and course?

   d. Time and stress suggested for content objectives?

   e. Resources identified for objectives and activities?

   f. Instructional strategies suggested for specific objectives?

3. Alignment of the curriculum: Is there congruence between written, tested, and taught curriculum?

4. Timeliness and currency of the curriculum: Is there a periodic review of the curriculum?

5. Direction and resource use: Does the board approve and adopt the curriculum and materials?

6. Validity and appropriateness of curriculum content: Is this the *right* curriculum content?

Exhibit 7.7. Curriculum Design Policy Issues for Quality Improvement

Three things have to be decided about curriculum content: (a) What should be included? (b) How much emphasis or time should be provided? (c) How shall the content be sequenced? Obviously, not everything can be included, because knowledge is immense and time is limited. Issues for the board in the area of curriculum content and design to consider in policy development are listed in Exhibit 7.7 (English, 1993).

Policy direction from the board on curriculum content issues is an essential ingredient in the quality improvement process.

- Predictability and congruity of the written curriculum from one level to another: Is the "flow" from grade to grade articulated in a smooth, coherent manner?

- Horizontal coordination of the written curriculum from school to school across grade levels: Are the levels of curriculum comparable from classroom to classroom across the system?

- Training for the staff in implementation of the curriculum: Are faculty and staff properly supported with training in delivering the programs and services of the system?

- Monitoring of the curriculum: Does the administration assure compliance with the policy and curriculum guidelines for the system within all school units?

- Equitable access to the curriculum: Are all educational opportunities of the system provided fairly, justly, and consistently to all clients and customers?

- Connectivity: Are resources allocated to areas of greatest need, and do teachers and administrators respond to school policies and priorities over time?

- Instructional efficacy: Are instruction and educational practices effective in nature and process, and is there provision for individual client differences and needs?

Exhibit 7.8. Curriculum Delivery Policy Issues for Quality Improvement

Curriculum Implementation and Delivery

Actual implementation and delivery of the curriculum is no less important than its design. Even in cases of high-quality curriculum design, failure to implement curriculum properly can suboptimize the organization's efforts at quality improvement. Delivery of curriculum includes a number of policy-related issues for board consideration that are spelled out in Exhibit 7.8.

1. Scope and quality of assessment: What elements of organizational functioning are assessed and under what conditions?
2. Data use in organizational improvement efforts: What types of information are most useful and helpful in effecting improvement of quality throughout the system, and how are they used?
   a. Can programs be examined in terms of desired learner results?
   b. Is it possible to give feedback to teaching staff so as to improve classroom effectiveness?
   c. Can strengths and weaknesses of various programs and services be compared?
3. Monitoring organizational progress: Is the board able to determine the effectiveness of organizational programs and services over time and to modify or to terminate ineffective organizational activities?

Exhibit 7.9. Assessment Policy Issues for Quality Improvement

Curriculum delivery must reflect the system's goals and manifest the purposes of the organization in order to be "connected." Roles and responsibilities require definition and structured descriptions that undergird delivery of the curriculum in ways that accomplish the desired ends of the system and that contribute to continuous quality improvement.

Assessment of Organizational Performance

Stressed earlier in this text was the essentialness of feedback on organizational performance. Without some idea of how the organization is doing, the board would be hard-pressed to know whether or not the aims and purposes of the system are being achieved. Assessment is necessary in substantive amount and useful form to effect quality improvement. Policy issues that are relevant to feedback and assessment are delineated in Exhibit 7.9.

- Defined roles and responsibilities: Are policies, procedures, and relationships clearly established and understood by all people involved in the organization?
- Skills and training: Are the needs of workers consistently met in support of organizational movement toward quality improvement?
- Rewards and penalties: Are intrinsic motivational processes established and maintained congruently?
- Communication: Is rationale for change and improvement shared widely across the system?
- Quality processes: Are the organization's defined purposes matching up with the vision and values of the people in the system?
- Balance of human needs: Is there a balance between people's need for individual expression and the need to be part of a team?
- Relationships and valence: Is collegiality evident throughout the system beyond congeniality, are groups working effectively as teams, and are relationships positive or negative?

Exhibit 7.10. Human Resources Policy Issues for Quality Improvement

Without adequate assessment, decision making is reduced to speculation and nonrational decision making. The quality improvement process requires a timely and appropriate foundation of system performance information that can be used to analyze organizational performance and help decision making directed at improvement of quality.

Human Resources and Relationships

People make the organization go or not go. All efforts at improvement succeed or fail depending on a number of factors, nearly all of which involve people and relationships. The obvious

- Congruence among curriculum objectives, results, and costs: Is there a tangible relationship between the programs and services needed and the allocation of resources?

- Demonstrated support and environmental provisions for organizational purpose: Are environments conducive to organizational purposes, and is there efficient and facilitating support for instruction throughout the system?

- Interventions to improve performance within existing limitations: Are allocations a product of measured results of performance, and are resources provided for growth and improvement processes?

- Involvement and responsibility: Are those responsible for implementing the work of the system to achieve system goals involved in decision making and resource allocations?

- Adequacy and prioritization: Are resources allocated based on cooperatively developed priorities in configurations based on criticality of need and relationship to organizational effectiveness?

Exhibit 7.11. Productivity Policy Issues for Quality Improvement

organizational relationships have been addressed elsewhere in this text; that is, superintendent-board, but other relationships merit board attention and consideration. Most of the literature on quality improvement discusses the implications of change on people (Scherkenbach, 1991). However, changing people is still no easy task. Several policy issues for boards to consider in human resources and relationships are listed in Exhibit 7.10.

The message of quality improvement must line up with the practices and actual behavior of the organization. Conflicts between what is said and what is done in an organization inhibit quality improvement substantially. Interdependent systems, such as schools, can achieve their goals in both cooperative or competitive ways. In quality improvement systems, cooperation and caring emphasize in deed what the organization seeks in word.

Material Resources and Productivity

Productivity is the relationship between input and output. The effective school system must find ways to deliver more effective instruction and at the same time find ways to operate more efficiently with limited resources. As a consequence of the need to improve even with limited or less resources, productivity becomes a high priority. There are a number of issues that are relevant for board policy consideration in the area of resources and productivity (English, 1993; Poston, Stone, & Muther, 1992), and these are delineated in Exhibit 7.11.

To begin with, all programs and activities of the organization must be reviewed on the basis of both performance and cost by a cross-functional organizational team. Funding and allocations should be based on "How are we doing?" rather than on "How much did we spend last year?" Given programmatic focus and prioritization, organizational resources are used more efficiently, and organizational improvement is enhanced (Poston et al., 1992).

Summary

School system oversight is a major undertaking for a conscientious board. The role of the board involves providing constancy of purpose and focus on the customer, developing and establishing policy direction for the system, and monitoring system performance. Supervision of the superintendent requires a clear separation of duties, with the board dealing with ends and the superintendent being held accountable for the means of the organization. Elements of school system quality to be monitored for quality improvement contain curriculum content and design, curriculum delivery and implementation, assessment and measurement of all aspects of organizational functioning including criterion-based assessment of client achievement, human resources and relationships, and use of material resources. Board oversight responsibilities, properly executed, enhance system quality.

Key Terms and Concepts

Articulation. The vertical congruence within a school system's curriculum from grade to grade within content areas over time.

Coordination. The horizontal congruence within a school system's curriculum across and within schools, content areas, and classrooms.

Institutionalization. The never-ending process of incorporating changes into ongoing organizational activities and functions on a permanent basis.

Oversight. The actions and functions of the governing board in monitoring and evaluating the performance of the organization and the results from organizational operations and activities for future decision making and improvement.

References

Carver, J. (1990). *Boards that make a difference.* San Francisco: Jossey-Bass.

Ciampa, D. (1991). *Total quality.* New York: Addison-Wesley.

Deming, W. E. (1982) *Out of the crisis.* Cambridge: MIT Press.

Elliot, C. (1993). *1993 board member manual.* Frederick, MD: Aspen Publishers.

English, F. W. (1988). *Curriculum auditing.* Lancaster, PA: Technomic.

English, F. W. (1993). *Curriculum management audit training manual.* Arlington, VA: American Association of School Administrators.

Frase, L. E. (1993). Findings: Standard I. In L. E. Frase (Ed.), *A curriculum management audit of the Huntsville City Schools* (pp. 11-34). Arlington, VA: American Association of School Administrators, National Curriculum Audit Center.

Holt, M. (1993). The educational consequences of W. Edwards Deming. *Phi Delta Kappan, 74*(5), 382-388.

Nowakowski, J., & First, P. F. (1989). *A study of the impact of educational reform on the schools.* Normal: Illinois State University, Illinois Association for Supervision and Curriculum Development.

Organization for Economic Cooperation and Development. (1987). *Quality of schooling: A clarifying report* (Restricted Secretariat Paper ED[87] 13). Paris: Author.

Poston, W. K., Jr. (1994). Standard three: The connectivity and equity standard. In L. E. Frase (Ed.), *The curriculum audit and total quality management.* Lancaster, PA: Technomic.

Poston, W. K., Jr., Stone, P., & Muther, C. (1992). *Making schools work: Practical management of support operations.* Newbury Park, CA: Corwin Press.

Scherkenbach, W. W. (1991). *Deming's road to continual improvement.* Knoxville, TN: SPC Press.

Senge, P. (1990). *The fifth discipline.* New York: Doubleday.

Twentieth Century Fund Task Force. (1992). *Facing the challenge: The report of the Twentieth Century Fund Task Force on school governance.* New York: Twentieth Century Fund.

Wagner, R. F., Jr. (1992). The case for local education policy boards. *Phi Delta Kappan, 74*(3), 228-229.

✧ **8** ✧

Implementing TQE:
The Board's Challenge

Whatever quality a school system exhibits, it begins with the board. The people who choose to serve on school boards are as conscientious and selfless as a group of people could be in public service. For the most part, board members are made up of competent people who believe in schools as something they should support and serve, and they bring to the board a wealth of ideas, dreams, and hopes for improving schools. However, despite the members' high hopes, boards somehow get deflected from spending time reflecting, exploring, and clarifying their dreams. Instead, they spend inordinate amounts of their time on unimportant, even trivial, items (Carver, 1990).

Board members have recognized that their job has become clouded with management tasks, confused with demands from all sides, and consumed with tasks that take a lot of time but give little benefit in return. (Twentieth Century Fund Task Force, 1992). Survival of local governing boards as we know them has been called into question, and communities across the nation have given boards a stinging vote of no confidence. Boards can continue to govern school systems and do it effectively, but not without substantial change in the way they do business. Unless substantial transformation is effected, boards may go out of business as a natural consequence of failure to meet customer needs and to assure quality in a system. Governing boards must redefine their role and redesign their responsibilities to truly impact organizational performance and to bring quality improvement to life in their school organizations. Specific quality improvement suggestions for boards are presented in this chapter.

Dimensions of Board Competencies in Quality Improvement

Some boards are more effective than others. Dimensions of effectiveness that differ markedly from the usual conceptions of board performance have been suggested by comprehensive studies of board members' beliefs about key ingredients of effectiveness (Chait, Holland, & Taylor, 1993). Six competencies and their dimensions are enumerated in Exhibit 8.1.

Boards that focus on the above dimensions have already begun the quest for quality improvement, and their effectiveness is likely to be evident within the school system and across the board's constituency. The board's effectiveness also depends in large part on how well it shares power with its executive officer.

Leadership Empowerment for Quality Improvement

Effective management and leadership is essential in quality improvement, This means that the board must set up the mechanisms for leadership to grow and flourish. Leadership succeeds in an environment of trust and freedom to not only make decisions but to make mistakes as well. The tendency for boards to intervene in system operations and to "micromanage" causes them to become immersed in day-to-day organizational activities that are better handled by the professional administrator designated by the board to run the organization within the boundaries established by board policy. Boards must become policy boards instead of "collective management" committees (Twentieth Century Fund Task Force, 1992).

1. Contextual dimension: The board understands the system's mission, tradition, and history, and the board's behaviors are congruent with system values.

2. Educational dimension: The board emphasizes the need to learn, to seek feedback on performance, and to provide opportunities for board member education and development.

3. Interpersonal dimension: The board nurtures its own development as a group, establishes group goals and consciously attends to the board's collective strength and internal relationships.

4. Intellectual dimension: The board recognizes complexities and tolerates ambiguities, and it understands how different issues, actions, and decisions affect each other. The board also sees itself as one constituency among many.

5. Political dimension: The board respects and guards the integrity of the governance process, avoids win-lose situations, and accepts as one of its primary responsibilities the need to build healthy relationships with all clientele.

6. Strategic dimension: The board directs its attention to a limited number of priorities or decisions identified as having strategic or symbolic importance to the system.

Exhibit 8.1. Competencies Associated with Board Effectiveness

Boards rightfully are responsible for setting broad policy guidelines for the organization, conducting oversight of the system, defining and demanding accountability, and providing planning for long-term direction. Most important, the wise board stays out of management activity, allowing its chosen leader to lead the organization. Meddling in school operations makes no one but the board accountable for mistakes and/or successes. The board must empower its chief executive officer to run the system toward the board-established ends and goals and support the superintendent's efforts within board-established limitations. Getting embroiled in the details of how ends are to be met causes the board to obstruct its primary obligation in leadership. The board's ability to empower and trust its chosen leader to manage the organization is witness to its own ability to govern effectively.

Improving Team Effectiveness in Quality Improvement

Teams are powerful forces in effecting change, and team involvement produces significant benefits. It fosters better decision making, enables ownership and implementation efforts, and capitalizes on intrinsic motivation (Deming, 1982). A board that is working well as a team is a board that is contributing to quality.

Interpersonal Dimensions

The board is a group. It must work as a group, it must make decisions as a group, and it can only grow and develop as a group. Little or no benefit accrues to a collection of individuals unless they nurture their collective strength as a team. Teams are better equipped to tackle complex, difficult problems and to create constructive, workable solutions. The interaction within a team also motivates—working together productively on important governance issues generates enthusiasm and esprit de corps, even during tough times. Team building is aided by certain personal behaviors, which are listed in Exhibit 8.2.

An individual board member can only do so much to improve a system, but pooling talents, know-how, and perspectives of board members as a team can contribute to major gains in quality improvement.

Meetings in Quality Improvement

Board meetings are simultaneously opportunities for a bane or a boon. Meetings can accomplish a huge job with a small amount of time (Carver, 1990). However, economy of time requires effectiveness in planning and conducting meetings. Board meetings also are the stage on which divergent board points of view are

- Shows a willingness to share relevant points of view clearly to the team for mutual understanding
- Treats fellow team members with sensitivity and extends relationships within the team to other situations and opportunities
- Actively listens to other team members to gain insight and understanding
- Openly and routinely accepts opportunities to agree and disagree with others on the team, without malice or carryover to other issues
- Participates constructively in helping the team to function as a group and to succeed
- Focuses on ideas, proposed suggestions, and determination of the consequences of ideas, without impugning or attacking other team members or their motivation
- Works for genuine consensus and supports team decisions once made

Exhibit 8.2. Personal Characteristics of a Team Contributor

welded into a unified, clear voice for the organization. Without a coherent, clear voice of organizational purpose set and conveyed by the board, quality improvement is stillborn.

MAXIMIZING QUALITY THROUGH MEETINGS

Is a meeting necessary? If so, what are the meeting's purpose and desired outcomes? Who should attend the meeting? What is the sequence and content of the agenda? The answers to these four questions form the basis for any meeting. The first question depends on several factors, including those revealed in Exhibit 8.3.

Determining the purpose and the desired outcomes of the meeting is helpful before the board meets. Many things come to boards that need not come to them in the first place. If the matter presented for action is a matter that belongs to any employee, then the matter is best referred to the superintendent. Everything that

1. The issues are clearly within board responsibility and discretion.
   a. Deal with organizational purposes or expectations.
   b. Require board action or processing.
   c. Clarify or determine executive and board relationships or constraints.
2. Not all board members have sufficient understanding of issues, and information is best communicated in a group meeting.
3. The board as a whole is required to act or make a decision.
   a. Conflicting views need to be reconciled.
   b. Group deliberations can only handle the matters at issue.
   c. Time and energy of the board will not be wasted.

Exhibit 8.3. Factors to Determine Necessity of Meetings

is not clearly a function of the board's governance responsibility (ends, policies, organizational limitations, or board relationships) "belongs" to the superintendent. If the issue clearly belongs to the board, then a meeting can be planned and conducted. However, expectations for the agenda should be established, but good agendas only include those things that must be done by the board and only the board (Carver, 1990). Quality factors in meetings include the items enumerated in Exhibit 8.4.

A well-planned meeting contains only essential items, avoids entanglement with administrative responsibilities, and includes well-stated meeting outcomes. Clearly established agenda outcomes provide common expectations among all board members, fix the limits of the meeting, and provide the means to assure a relationship with organizational quality or productivity (Kayser, 1990). If the board does not function as the "navigator of the ship" in setting direction for its schools, the schools will probably always be off course.

1. Group interaction capitalizes on human resources.
2. The group focuses its activities on defined outcomes for the meeting.
3. Performance data undergird decision making aimed at improvement over time.
4. Policy development avoids repetitive decision making and economizes time.
5. Greater ownership and creativity come from collaborative power.
6. People feel their ideas and contributions count for something.
7. All group members participate and put forth a mutually supportive environment.
8. Divergent viewpoints without rancor stimulate creative thinking and are encouraged.
9. Conflicts are constructively reconciled.
10. Final decisions are supported by the group in order to facilitate executive action.

Exhibit 8.4. Quality Factors in Board Meetings

Maintaining Board Focus on Quality

Board behavior affects the overall performance of the school organization. What the board models in its behavior sends a very powerful message throughout the system, as to what is important and what merits priority. The time and energies of the board are best used to address certain elements of functioning, including purpose, planning, people, and priorities.

Standards for Quality Improvement

In quality improvement, there is no substitute for board leadership in creating values for the school organization and incorporating those values into the way the system functions. Moreover, the board is a key in maintaining public support and credibility by virtue of how it projects its organizational values to the community and to clientele. The board sets the pace for quality improvement. The Malcolm C. Baldrige National Quality Award sets seven comprehensive standards for industry in quality improvement (Ciampa, 1992), and those standards applied to schools are listed in Exhibit 8.5.

Quality begins with intent, and intent is fixed by management (Deming, 1982). The importance of the board is underscored in Deming's personal belief that quality improvement goes nowhere without top leadership's involvement and commitment (Richter, 1993). Moreover, given the changes and challenges confronting schools today, unless the board makes quality improvement work in its system, schools as configured today will become irrelevant in the world of tomorrow.

Putting Quality Improvement in Place

Where should the board start? There are significant volumes on implementing quality extant in professional literature, but making sense of the overwhelming amount of information is difficult. Knowing where to start would give constructive guidance to a board that is interested in quality improvement.

START WITH VISION AND PLANNING

Boards should start putting quality improvement in place by first dealing with vision and clarification of what the organization stands for. This involves asking three questions:

1. What business are we really in?
2. How can we know if we are successful?
3. How can we get better?

Long-term thinking is essential. Short-term thinking is like cramming for an examination: It takes care of the need for a quick remedy but does little in assuring the long-term good (Covey, 1989). Deming says organizations are like big ships running at full

1. Leadership (100 points)
   a. The board is personally involved and visible in maintaining an environment for quality improvement.
   b. System values are communicated throughout the system and are reflected in how the system operates.
   c. The superintendent integrates quality values into day-to-day management and operations of all system units.
   d. The system extends itself to the external community as a model for safe, ethical, and credible educational practices.
2. Information and analysis (70 points)
   a. The board and the superintendent use and manage data and information of wide scope and sound validity in quality improvement processes.
   b. Adequate data and analyses support prevention-based approaches to quality, and customer satisfaction is built on solid information and feedback.
3. Strategic quality planning (60 points)
   a. Long-range planning is integrated into all major components of organizational operations to achieve and maintain quality leadership.
4. Human resource utilization (150 points)
   a. The board and superintendent's primary concern is benefits for people, characterized by full participation in continuous improvement.
   b. Full personal and organizational growth is fostered and supported by training and development aimed at improvement.
5. Quality assurance of services and programs (140 points)
   a. Measurement and assessment tools are used for design and delivery of programs and services.
   b. Processes are continually examined for ways and means for improvement in all areas.

Exhibit 8.5. Standards for Quality in School Systems

6. Quality results (180 points)

a. Objective evidence demonstrates customer requirements and expectations are being met or exceeded in educational and support operations.

7. Customer satisfaction (300 points)

a. The system demonstrates adequate knowledge of its customers, responsiveness to customer needs and requirements, and ability to meet or surpass customer requirements and expectations.

Total points: 1000 points

Exhibit 8.5. Continued

speed: They take a lot of time and substantial distance to turn. As a part of planning, an analysis of strengths and weaknesses will prevent the board from implementing quality improvement before it is ready. If the organization's current culture and character is in question, a quality audit is recommended to see how the system can embrace quality improvement.

BECOME OBSESSED WITH AIMS AND PURPOSES

"Passion, commitment, and fire for what we are doing must start at (the board) table," pleaded one governance official (Carver, 1990, p. 193). The board must focus on the values and ends of the system. Working to keep the purposes and mission of the system out-front, the board can keep its dreams and hopes for a quality organization alive. Competing viewpoints and divergent ideas are the fabric of powerful organizational purposes and worthwhile goals. Fear must be eliminated throughout the organization to mobilize the best suggestions of all people concerned.

Ownership of goals and purposes will work only with the collaboration and involvement of all employees and significant stakeholders. Remember that people who are closest to the work are the best experts available for what it takes to make the system succeed.

MODEL DIRECT INVOLVEMENT

Direct involvement of the board and top management is critical for success. Teachers have seen a lot of programs come and go—any program could go the same way. Board commitment and involvement will show that this process is different and that quality improvement is a new way of doing business. When the board and the superintendent team become involved in something, and they are observed by the organization expending effort to make it work, serious commitment is obvious.

The past behavior of the system should be viewed as a foundation for the future, not a picture of failure. Change is beneficial if the change (a) represents a pursuit of quality, (b) results from recognition that any organization can get better, or (c) reflects a belief that quality begins from the top with the board.

SHARE RESPONSIBILITY FOR QUALITY

Total Quality Education is based on the collaboration of everyone in the system. People want to contribute, but they also want to feel that their contributions are significant and valued. Partnerships with all organizational players recognize that people want input on what affects them and their job. People want to know that they are heard, understood, and considered in the improvement process. If collaboration extends up and down through the entire organization, quality improvement can be deployed throughout the entire school system.

INVEST IN TRAINING AND DEVELOPMENT

Two of Deming's 14 principles of quality address the need for training (Points 6 and 13—see chapter 2). It is critical to recognize that none of us is better than our current capability, but our current capability can be increased or improved. Training and development programs and opportunities, including programs for the board itself, yield immense returns to the organization. Learning new knowledge should be viewed as an organizational asset, and investments in training and development offer substantial returns.

Not everybody is prepared to implement quality improvement, and training should focus on building employee confidence in continuous improvement and fostering motivation to become involved in the process. The hallmark of a viable organization is its character of commitment to continuously learning how it can improve (Senge, 1990).

CONTINUALLY REINVENT QUALITY

Quality is a journey, not a destination. The process of empowerment and employee involvement for quality improvement is a powerful process—once unleashed, it never ends. The board must provide a positive and supportive environment for change, and it must demonstrate trust in the process of employee involvement. If things are not working properly, fix them. Fix them without trying to point blame at anyone. The system is to blame—the system needs to be fixed (Deming, 1982).

Schools have been notoriously resistant to change over their history, but the board must show that it believes in the process of quality improvement and that the process of improvement is valued. Employees must be able to use data and performance information to see how things are working, to make real changes in their work processes, and to implement their improvements. There is opportunity for change, and quality is always subject to improvement. As once said, "If it ain't broke, you just haven't looked hard enough" (Peters, 1988, p. 3). Anything good can get better.

Board Dedication to Quality
Improvement: A Closing Thought

As this book draws to a close, the urgency of emphasizing the board's role and responsibilities becomes increasingly important. Basically, Total Quality Education may be the last best hope for public schooling institutions in America, and boards are the governing bodies that can make it happen. Perhaps the best way to close would be to suggest that each board member reading this consider *kaizen*, or what the Japanese call "dedication to continuous improvement."

If this attribute were to be found in our school systems, our boards would show constant dedication to quality improvement, not only for the systems and their schools but also for themselves and in all relationships throughout the community. Policies would value the worth of people and process, create learning environments, reflect system thinking, incorporate information into work and purpose enhancement, and results would delight customers. A zeal for learning and growing and improving would be contagious, and the spirit of *kaizen* would permeate every corner of our school organization. That is a future worth creating.

Key Terms and Concepts

Empowerment. An environment of trust and freedom to make decisions (and mistakes) without intervention from higher levels within an organization consistently over time.

Quality standards. A set of seven elements of organizational functioning used in determining the level of quality within the organization dealing with leadership, planning, information use, human resources, assessment, and customer satisfaction.

References

Carver, J. (1990). *Boards that make a difference: A new design for leadership in nonprofit and public organizations.* San Francisco: Jossey-Bass.

Chait, R. P., Holland, T. P., & Taylor, B. E. (1993). *The effective board of trustees.* Phoenix, AZ: American Council on Education, Oryx Press.

Ciampa, D. (1992). *Total quality: A user's guide for implementation.* New York: Addison-Wesley.

Covey, S. (1989). *The seven habits of highly effective people.* New York: Simon & Schuster.

Deming, W. E. (1982). *Out of the crisis.* Cambridge: MIT Press.

Kayser, T. A. (1990). *Mining group gold: How to cash in on the collaborative brain power of a group.* El Segundo, CA: Serif Publishing (Xerox).

Peters, T. J. (1988). *Thriving on chaos: Handbook for a management revolution.* New York: Knopf.

Richter, K. (1993, September). *Chevron Corporation's quality improvement program and school implications.* Paper presented to faculty and staff of the Algona Community School District, Algona, IA.

Senge, P. M. (1990). *The fifth discipline.* New York: Doubleday.

Twentieth Century Fund Task Force. (1992). *Facing the challenge: The report of the Twentieth Century Fund Task Force on school governance.* New York: Twentieth Century Fund.

Planning and Troubleshooting Guide

In compliance with GPSR, should you have any concerns about the safety of this product, please advise: International Associates Auditing & Certification Limited The Black Church, St Mary's Place, Dublin 7, D07 P4AX Ireland EUAR@ie.ia-net.com